ROUTLEDGE LIBRARY EDITIONS:
LORD BYRON

Volume 7

AT THE TITAN'S BREAKFAST

AT THE TITAN'S BREAKFAST
Three Essays on Byron's Poetry

ROBERT POLITO

LONDON AND NEW YORK

First published in 1987 by Garland Publishing, Inc.

This edition first published in 2016
by Routledge
2 Park Square, Milton Park, Abingdon, Oxon OX14 4RN

and by Routledge
711 Third Avenue, New York, NY 10017

Routledge is an imprint of the Taylor & Francis Group, an informa business

© 1987 Robert Polito

All rights reserved. No part of this book may be reprinted or reproduced or utilised in any form or by any electronic, mechanical, or other means, now known or hereafter invented, including photocopying and recording, or in any information storage or retrieval system, without permission in writing from the publishers.

Trademark notice: Product or corporate names may be trademarks or registered trademarks, and are used only for identification and explanation without intent to infringe.

British Library Cataloguing in Publication Data
A catalogue record for this book is available from the British Library

ISBN: 978-1-138-67557-5 (Set)
ISBN: 978-1-315-56060-1 (Set) (ebk)
ISBN: 978-1-138-67323-6 (Volume 7) (hbk)
ISBN: 978-1-138-67324-3 (Volume 7) (pbk)
ISBN: 978-1-315-56207-0 (Volume 7) (ebk)

Publisher's Note
The publisher has gone to great lengths to ensure the quality of this reprint but points out that some imperfections in the original copies may be apparent.

Disclaimer
The publisher has made every effort to trace copyright holders and would welcome correspondence from those they have been unable to trace.

AT THE TITAN'S BREAKFAST

Three Essays on Byron's Poetry
ROBERT POLITO

Garland Publishing, Inc.
New York & London
1987

Copyright © 1987 by Robert Polito

All Rights Reserved

Library of Congress Cataloging-in-Publication Data
Polito, Robert, 1951-
At the titan's breakfast.

(Harvard dissertations in American and English literature)
Thesis (Ph.D.) — Harvard University, 1981.
Bibliography: p.
Contents: When fierce conflicting passions urge — Disporting there like any other fly — At the titan's breakfast.
1. Byron, George Gordon Byron, Baron, 1788-1824 — Criticism and interpretation.   I. Title.   II. Series.
PR4388.P637   1987   821'.7   87-19661
ISBN 0-8240-0072-2

The volumes in this series are printed on acid-free, 250-year-life paper.
Printed in the United States of America

At the Titan's Breakfast:

Three Essays on Byron's Poetry

A thesis presented

by

Robert Joseph Polito

to

The Department of English and American Literature and Language

in partial fulfillment of the requirements
for the degree of
Doctor of Philosophy
in the subject of

English

Harvard University
Cambridge, Massachusetts

October, 1981

In memory of Mark Gibbons and Joseph Polito

Table of Contents

Acknowledgments   3

I.   When Fierce Conflicting Passions Urge   5
II. Disporting There Like Any Other Fly   95
III. At the Titan's Breakfast   155

Notes   189
Bibliography   192

Acknowledgements

I wish to thank Brooke Hopkins, Mary Lee, Sarah Minden, David Perkins, and Margaret Polito. For their assistance and support in the preparation of this thesis, for their kindness and generosity--various yet constant--I shall always be grateful.

I also wish to acknowledge the generous assistance of the Ingram Merrill Foundation, which supported my study of Byron's _Childe Harold_.

I

When Fierce Conflicting Passions Urge

The poems that Byron published in his four early books of poetry, <u>Fugitive Pieces</u>, <u>Poems on Various Occasions</u>, <u>Hours of Idleness</u>, and <u>Poems Original and Translated</u> were written at an unusually young age, even for English poets of the early nineteenth century. But apart from the dates of composition that follow every poem, bringing each to an end with an efficient click, or the significant debts this writing owes to the reading of its author--Lord Strangford, Thomas Moore, Burns, Pope,--and the many uncertainties in diction and tone, there is remarkably little in the poems themselves that identifies them as the work of a young man. In poem after poem we find the speaker discussing his life as if it were over. Frequently he is about to die ("The Adieu"), or wishes that he were dead already: "Oh! when shall the grave hide forever my sorrow," ("To Caroline").[1] He has no family, contrary to his letters ("Childish Recollections"). All of his friends have died, or have left him behind ("Stanzas"). And he does not expect to fall in love again ("To Romance"). The present, typically, is "hell," and for the future, "the coming tomorrow/But brings with new torture, the curse of today" ("To Caroline").

What pleasure he does find is in dreams,

> "Oft in the progress of some fleeting dream,
> Fraternal smiles, collected round me seem,
> While still the visions to my heart are prest,
> The voice of Love will murmur in my rest;"
>   ("Childish Recollections," 11.229-232)

and above all in returning to scenes of his seemingly distant past: "I ask but this--again to rove/Through scenes my

youth hath known before." ("Song") But these memories
rarely have any sustaining power, or bring him escape, or
even respite. Most often they are a source of pain and
regret. In "On a Distant View of the Village and School,
of Harrow, on the Hill" he writes: "Ye scenes of my childhood, whose lov'd recollection/Embitters the present, compared with the past." And always he is alone: "As the last
of my race I must wither alone." ("Song") The version of
the much revised "Childish Recollections" that appeared in
Poems on Various Occasions contains these lines:

> "Weary of love, of life, devour'd with spleen,
> I rest, a perfect Timon, not nineteen;
> World! I renounce thee! all my hope's o'ercast;
> One sigh I give thee, but that sigh's the last,
> Friends, foes, and females, now alike, adieu!
> Would I could add, remembrance of you, too.
> Yet, though the future, dark and cheerless gleams,
> The curse of memory, hovering in my dreams,
> Depicts, with glowing pencil, all those years,
> Ere yet, my cup, empoison'd flow'd, with tears,
> Still rules my senses with tyrannic sway,
> The past confounding with the present day.
>
> Alas! in vain I check the maddening thought,
> It still recurs, unlook'd for, and unsought;"
>   POVO (ll.15-28)

The emphases here are Childe Harold's (whom Byron once described as "a modern Timon"),[2] and indeed that "wandering
outlaw of his own dark mind" seems to have had a hand in com-
posing many of Byron's early poems. There is a misplaced
excitement in this passage that, perhaps, renders it bathetic,
and marks it, like "The Tear," for The Stuffed Owl. But
the attitudes expressed here, and the conclusions the speaker
has reached about his life, are entirely representative of
the poems which Byron wrote before 1809; and many parallel

passages, more controlled and pointed usually, can be found in <u>Childe Harold</u>, <u>Don Juan</u>, and in virtually all of his later collections. Yeats in "The Bounty of Sweden" writes that after the ceremony in which he was awarded the Nobel Prize had concluded, his first desire was to be alone, so that he could linger over his medal:

> "All is over, and I am able to examine my medal, a work of charming, decorative, academic design, French in manner, a work of the 'nineties. It shows a young man listening to a Muse, who stands young and beautiful with a great lyre in her hand, and I think as I examine it, 'I was good-looking like that young man, but my unpractised verse was full of infirmity, my Muse old as it were; and now I am old and rheumatic, and nothing to look at, but my Muse is young."[3]

The Muse of Byron's early "unpractised verse" is also "old as it were." But unlike Yeats's, it remained "old," even as his control over his poetry increased, until the end of his life. The affinity Yeats observes between the design of the medal and the style of his early poetry--"charming, decorative, academic design, French in manner"--is deft both as wit and as criticism. But the suggestion in his phrase, "a work of the 'nineties," that the "infirmity" of his verse was a learned affectation, partaking of the melancholy that has been fashionable with young poets not just in the 'nineties, but for at least two centuries, and a posture to be outgrown, does not really apply to Byron. In this respect, all of his poetry, early and late, is of a piece.

The attitude that Byron's "old" Muse strikes in the lines I have just quoted is a grand weariness, rendered in the voice of one who believes that he has experienced everything: "Weary of love, of life, devour'd with spleen,/I rest, a perfect Timon, not nineteen." Like Timon's, the misanthropy here is democratic and all embracing: "Friends, foes, and females, now alike, adieu!" And like Shakespeare's Athenian lord, he is haunted by his past--"The past confounding with the present day"--which "hovers" over him like a "curse," and wishes only to forget: "Alas! in vain I check the maddening thought,/It still recurs, unlook'd for and unsought." A later section in the same version of "Childish Recollections" returns to these matters, at once fleshing them out with particulars and alluding to even larger areas of experience.

> "Ah! vain endeavour, in this childish strain,
> To soothe the woes, of which I thus complain,
> What can avail this fruitless loss of time,
> To measure sorrow, in a jingling rhyme!
> No social solace, from a friend, is near,
> And heartless strangers drop no feeling tear.
> I seek not joy, in woman's sparkling eye,
> The smiles of beauty cannot check the sigh.
> Adieu! thou world! thy pleasure's still a dream,
> Thy virtue, but a visionary theme;
> Thy years of vice, on years of folly roll,
> 'Till grinning death assigns the destin'd goal;
> Where all are hastening to the dread abode,
> To meet the judgement of a righteous God;
> Mix'd in the concourse of the thoughtless throng,
> A mourner, 'midst of mirth, I glide along;
> A wretched, isolated, gloomy thing,
> Curst by reflection's deep corroding sting:
>
> . . .
>
> Not crimes I mourn; but happiness gone by.
> Thus, crawling on with many a reptile vile,
> My heart is bitter, though my cheek may smile;
> No more, with former bliss, my breast is glad,
> Hope yields to anguish, and my soul is sad:
> From fond regret, no future joy can save,
> Remembrance slumbers only in the grave."
>
> POVO (ll.361-378; 406-412)

Again the sentiments point to a pervasive world-weariness,

and many of the same bells are rung, if for a longer time. The brief reference to "friends, foes, and females" in the earlier passage is here expanded to six lines, with a corresponding increase in bitterness as well. Similarly, the world that he was perfunctorily "weary" of above is now imagined as a haven of deceit, vice, folly, and energetic, self-destructive ignorance:

> "Adieu! thou world! Thy pleasure's still a dream,
> Thy virtue, but a visionary theme;
> Thy years of vice, on years of folly roll,
> 'Till grinning death assigns the destin'd goal;
> When all are hastening to the dread abode..."

Once more remembrance is a source of pain and "regret," and is maddeningly out of the speaker's control: "Remembrance slumbers only in the grave." The self-referential lines are perhaps of greater significance. The literary allusion to Timon (though both passages glance at Shakespeare's play, Act IV, <u>passim</u>, but especially, IV.i.11.1-40, IV.iii.11.249-276, and 11.374-392) has given way to a more direct expression of anguish and isolation:

> "A mourner, 'midst of mirth, I glide along;
> A wretched, isolated, gloomy thing,
> Curst by reflection's deep corroding sting..."

Previously, the poem considered the "Curse of Memory"; here the agent of the curse is "reflection," a word that includes the earlier sense, but passes beyond it to other mental activities, including those that figure in the writing of this poem. Indeed, "Childish Recollections" joins the many victims of "reflection's deep corroding sting." The passage began with a wistful questioning of its author's immediate procedures:

> "Ah! vain endeavor, in this childish strain,
> To soothe the woes, of which I thus complain;
> What can avail this fruitless loss of time,
> To measure sorrow, in a jingling rhyme!"

"Curst by reflection's deep corroding sting," the speaker's weariness and skepticism expands to include the very means by which he recognizes and expresses his weariness and skepticism.

A phrase that George Orwell used to characterize the generation of writers who came to prominence in England after the First World War defines precisely the posture that Byron promotes in this poem, and in the bulk of his early poems. Their "keynote," Orwell writes in his essay "Inside the Whale," is the sense that these writers "see through" all systems and ideals under which their predecessors had enlisted themselves.[4] The speaker of the lines I have quoted from "Childish Recollections" is not just, as I wrote above, someone who believes that he has experienced everything; he believes that he "sees through" it all as well.

In the pages that follow, I shall describe the strategies that Byron's "old Muse" elaborated in these early poems for registering and dramatizing her skepticism, for "seeing through" everything. Fortunately for the poems, this skepticism is not at all a rigid or static quality, as predictable and systematic in its way as any other creed. As he writes in Don Juan:

> "So little do we know what we're about in
> This world, I doubt if doubt itself be doubting."[5]

II

Byron's most dashing account of his skepticism appears at the beginning of Canto XIV of *Don Juan*.

> 1
> "If from great Nature's or our own abyss
>   Of thought we could but snatch a certainty,
> Perhaps mankind might find the path they miss,
>   But then 'twould spoil much good philosophy.
> One system eats another up, and this
>   Much as old Saturn ate his progeny,
> For when his pious consort gave him stones
> In lieu of sons, of these he made no bones.
>
> 2
> But System doth reverse the Titan's breakfast
>   And eats her parents, albeit the digestion
> Is difficult, Pray tell me, can you make fast
>   After due search your faith to any question?
> Look back o'er ages ere unto the stake fast
>   You bind yourself and call some mode the best one.
> Nothing more true than not to trust your senses,
> And yet what are your other evidences?
>
> 3
> For me, I know nought. Nothing I deny,
>   Admit, reject, contemn; and what know you,
> Except perhaps that you were born to die?
>   And both may after all turn out untrue.
> An age may come, font of eternity,
>   When nothing shall be either old or new.
> Death, so called, is a thing which makes men weep,
> And yet a third of life is passed in sleep."

This is among the most arresting passages in the poem, and as Jerome J. McGann writes, "it carries in itself the natural form of its total expression."[6] Every aspect of the style participates in the drama of the Titan's breakfast. The high Romantic seriousness of the first line, lofty and sublime, sinks a bit after the line-break, when we discover that the abyss is one "of thought," and even more in the third line with is depreciatory "perhaps," and its domestication of revelation as "find(ing) the path they miss." The "certainty" that might be "snatched" in the second line, after the fashion of a hero like Prometheus, turns out not to be especially desirable at all: "'twould spoil much good philosophy." The poem does not recognize that the value of a particular philosophy might be its access to truth. The same reluctance to consider belief reappears in the discussion of poetry which follows this passage.

> 7
> "But what's this to the purpose, you will say.
>   Gent. reader, nothing, a mere speculation,
> For which my sole excuse is, 'tis my way.
>   Sometimes with and sometimes without occasion
> I write what's uppermost without delay.
>   This narrative is not meant for narration,
> But a mere airy and fantastic basis
> To build up common things with commonplaces.
>
> 8
> You know, or don't know, that great Bacon saith,
>   'Fling up a straw, 'twill show the way the wind blows.'
> And such a straw, borne on by human breath,
>   Is poesy, according as the mind glows -
> A paper kite, which flies 'twixt life and death,
>   A shadow which the onward soul behind throws.
> And mine's a bubble not blown up for praise,
> But just to play with, as an infant plays.
>
> . . .
>
> 11
> But 'why then publish?' There are no rewards
>   Of fame or profit when the world grows weary.
> I ask in turn why do you play at cards?
>   Why drink? Why read? To make some hour less dreary.
> It occupies me to turn back regards
>   On what I've seen or pondered, sad or cheery,
> And what I write I cast upon the stream
> To swim or sink. I have had at least my dream."

Much good poetry would also be "spoiled" by "certainty," it seems. For both philosophy and poetry, Byron resists the claim of truth and "faith," and elevates other values, having to do with performance and play--"But just to play with, as infant plays." Don Juan is a conspicuously self-regarding performance; at every stage Byron is observing and evaluating his moment by moment participation in the activities and ideas he is setting down. Robert Frost once described his own poetic practice in terms that are particularly applicable to Byron's here. "What do I want to communicate but what a hell of a good time I had writing about it. The whole thing is performance and feats of association. Why don't critics talk about these things--what a feat it was to turn that way, and what a feat it was to remember that, to be reminded of that by this?"[7]

Central to Byron's performance is his rendition of a skeptical mind in motion, enacting in the line by line movement of his poem the historical processes he describes in the phrase, "One system eats another up." One of his more dramatic "feats of association" occurs in line 6 of the initial stanza, where he appropriates the myth of Saturn (usually Cronos) and Rhea for his own spectacularly unheroic purposes. The passage to this from the previous line is surprising and dazzling--"what a feat it was to remember that." The lines turn, I believe, on the words "eats" and "ate." When we first read "One system eats another up," the verb seems to mark only a casual, even silent metaphor; its return in the past tense in the next line suggests that there is more to it than this, that "eats" might be literally, perhaps grotesquely and repulsively, accurate. In this compact piece of wit, Byron confounds and questions his initial metaphor, drawing attention to the "violent" changes that regularly accompany the passing of one age's ideas to the next ("the digestion is difficult"), and to the real violence that often follows from strongly held beliefs. As he urges in the stanza that follows this,

> "Look back o'er ages ere onto the stake fast
> You bind yourself and call come mode the best one."

"Mode" is especially apt for Byron's purpose, implying that ideas, like hair or clothes, have their fashions, and come and go.

Characteristically, even after this unexpected application of the Greek myth, he does not let the matter rest. His language makes the Gods appear awfully small and domestic--"old Saturn," and his "pius consort" (hardly <u>pius Aeneas</u>). And immediately he goes on to qualify the story, turning it upside down:

> "But system doth reverse the Titan's breakfast
> And eats her parents, albeit the digestion
> Is difficult."

The skepticism is present everywhere in the writing of this passage--in the restless "buts," "and yets," in words like "albeit," "perhaps" and "except perhaps," in the interplay of high and low rhetorical styles, in the sly adoption of cliches (most notably "he makes no bones" at the end of the first stanza), and the rapid changes in perspective and point of view. Not even the powerful assertion of skepticism, toward which the entire passage has been building--

> "For me, I know nought. Nothing I deny,
> Admit, reject, contemn; and what know <u>you</u>,
> Except perhaps that you were born to die?"--

is allowed to pass unqualified, first by the nagging "perhaps," and then by the deadpan lines that complete the stanza.

> "And both may after all turn out untrue.
> An age may come, font of eternity,
> When nothing shall be either old or new.
> Death, so called, is a thing which makes men weep,
> And yet a third of life is passed in sleep."

No single poem in the early collections is as poised or confident as these lines; nowhere does Byron seem as comfortable and playful before his doubt and pessimism. And in none is the interweaving of subject matter and style quite as seamless and sophisticated. But in virtually all of the early poems we hear the same restless and active voice, attempting to make clear and direct statements, only to find that it cannot; as he writes, another idea or perspective occurs to him--"and yet"--and the original line must be qualified or undercut. Just as in these lines from Don Juan, at the center of Byron's early poems is some kind of conflict, a conflict that is never allowed to be resolved-- or if it is resolved in one poem, it is undone in another, often only a few pages away, or with a similar title. These poems express uncertainty, ambivalence, and above all a passionate interest in keeping many different aspects of a subject before us at the same time, and in developing other perspectives and alternate ways of perceiving and writing. The focus is always upon the speaker's own changing attitudes, his doubts and his uncertainties. Probably the essential characteristic of these early poems involves some change in perspective along the way, with the poem taking an unexpected turn or ending in a place that could not have been predicted from the title or the opening lines.

The verse forms that Byron employed in these lyrics, and many of the isolated sentiments, are often simple and conventional. But the final, total effect and expression is rarely so.

Here is a poem that did not appear in any of the early published collections (in fact, it was printed only in 1980). I choose it both because it was written so early--with the exception of a piece of doggerel titled "Epigram on an Old Lady Who had Some Curious Notions Respecting the Soul," it is Byron's first known poem--and because there seems to be so little to it.

Then Peace to Thy Spirit

"Then peace to thy spirit, my earliest Friend,
Beloved in thy life, and deplored in thine end;
Yet happy art thou to escape from the woe
Which awaits the survivors of friendship below.

I should not lament thee because thou art free
From the pangs that assail human nature and me;
Yet still I deplore thee in whom I have lost
The companion of childhood I valued the most.

Oh, if there is heaven thou surely art blest,
If death is eternal, at least then at rest.
Then away with the tears which we fruitlessly shed--
Let us mourne for the _living_, not weep for the dead.

Yet to think of the days we together have seen,
Of what thou now art, and of what we have been."

These sentiments on the passing of a young friend are thoroughly conventional, and have been derived to a significant degree from Thomas Moore's juvenile poems. Just as in the lines I quoted from Don Juan, we enter this sonnet very much in the middle of things; some internal debate has, presumably, been taking place, and what we are about to read is its conclusion--"Then peace." The speaker begins by stating how much he loved his friend in life, and how much he "deplored" his death. But these are really the only unconditional claims he makes in the poem; in the rest of it, he attempts other declarations and assertions, but finds that he must qualify them, endeavors to conclude, but is finally unable to. For instance, he keeps trying to state that his friend is better off now that he is dead:

> "Yet happy art thou to escape from the woe
> Which awaits the survivors of friendship below.
> I should not lament thee because thou art free
> From the pangs that assail human nature and me;"

And he keeps claiming that it is he and the dead friend's other companions who really should be mourned;

> "Oh, if there is heaven thou surely art blest,
> If death is eternal, at least then at rest.
> Then away with the tears which we fruitlessly shed--
> Let us mourne for the living, not weep for the dead."

His admonitions to himself are energetically phrased--"Then away with...," "I should not..."; and the contrast between the world in which the speaker has been left behind--full of "woe" and "pangs that assail"--and the one which his friend has gained--he has "escaped...from the woe which awaits," is "free from the pangs that assail," and if he is not "blest," he is at least "at rest"--is clearly defined, leaving the speaker no doubt about what his conclusion should be. But his restless active voice keeps resisting the claims he wishes to make:

> "Yet still I deplore thee in whom I have lost
> The companion of childhood I valued the most."

As in *Don Juan*, other perspectives enter the poem--the pleasure they found together in the past, his present pain--and prevent him from concluding, introduced here, as there, by the word "Yet." (This is one of the crucial words in Byron's early poetry, serving to introduce a change in perspective in at least twenty poems.) In the final couplet,

> "Yet to think of the days we together have seen,
> Of what thou now art, and of what we have been."

the speaker is back right where he started, still in the middle of things. The poem ends, but it does not conclude, the ringing couplet drawing greater attention to, perhaps even parodying, his inconclusiveness. At the finish, the speaker resides in a kind of eternal present, shaping strong assertions only to take them back, still full of conflicts, unable to grant peace either to his friend or to himself.

Another poem that involves a shift in perspective along the way, though a more unexpected and extreme one, is "To Caroline." Unlike "Then Peace to Thy Spirit," this poem is part of a series of four poems with the same title, which debate, as it were, different aspects of the same subjects. There are many such linked poems in these early collections which, when read together, often embody fierce contradictions. For example, "On Leaving Newstead Abbey," "Song" ("When I rov'd, a young Highlander, o'er the dark heath") and "Childish Recollections" offer forcibly differing accounts of his attitudes toward his ancestors and his family. In poems like "Oscar of Alva," "To a Knot of Ungenerous Critics," "The Death of Calmar and Orla" and "Soliloquy of a Bard in the Country," he emerges as a confident, even brash poet; yet in "Adieu to the Muse" he writes what he claims will be his last poem. "To the Duke of Dorset," "The Tear," "Pignus Amoris" and "To a Youthful Friend" all promote the Romantic identification of childhood with "Truth," while in "To Romance" childhood is a time of "deceit" and "affectation." Various aspects of love are celebrated or disparaged in "Stanzas to a Lady," "To M.S.G.," "To Mary on Receiving her Picture," "The First Kiss of Love," "Reply to Some Verses of J.M.B. Pigot, Esq.," "To the Sighing Strephon," "Love's Last Adieu," "To Romance," "To Mary," and "Remind Me Not." A number of other poems consider aspects of literary style: "To a Lady," "Lines Written in 'Letters of an Italian Nun and an English Gentleman'... Answer to the Foregoing, Address'd to Miss Pigot," "The First Kiss of Love," "Reply to Some Verses of J.M.B. Pigot, Esq.," and "To the Sighing Strephon." Finally, many poems debate questions involving the value of memory and recalling the past, "On Leaving Newstead Abbey," "To the Duke of Dorset," "To Emma," "Remembrance," "Song" ("When I rov'd a young Highlander, o'er the dark heath"), "To the Earl of Clare," "On a Distant View of the Village and School, of Harrow, on the Hill," "To a Beautiful Quaker," and, supremely, "Childish Recollections."

This list, long as it is, does not begin to illustrate definitively Byron's habit of constantly altering point of view, perspective, and attitude from poem to poem, dramatizing the contradictions and conflicts that shape the individual poems, but on a much larger scale. I begin with the "To Caroline" which was printed last in <u>Hours of Idleness</u>

(all were written about the same time, but their chronological order is unknown), because in addition to the concern with love, memory, language, and death that it shares with the others in the cycle, it contains its own rather strange shifts in perspective.

1.
"When I hear you express an affection so warm,
 Ne'er think, my belov'd, that I do not believe;
For your lip, would the soul of suspicion disarm,
 And your eye beams a ray, which can never deceive.

2.
Yet, still, this fond bosom regrets, whilst adoring,
 That love, like the leaf, must fall into the sear;
That age will come on, when remembrance deploring,
 Contemplates the scenes of her youth, with a tear.

3.
That the time must arrive, when, no longer retaining
 Their auburn, those locks must wave thin to the breeze;
When a few silver hairs of those tresses remaining,
 Prove nature a prey to decay and disease.

4.
'Tis this, my belov'd, which spreads gloom o'er my features,
 Tho' I ne'er shall presume to arraign the decree,
Which God has proclaim'd, as the fate of his creatures,
 In the death, which one day will deprive you of me.

5.
Mistake not, sweet sceptic, the cause of emotion,
 No doubt can the mind of your lover invade;
He worships each look, with such faithful devotion,
 A smile can enchant, or a tear can dissuade.

6.
But as death, my belov'd, soon or late, shall o'ertake us,
 And our breasts, which alive, with such sympathy glow,
Will sleep in the grave, till the blast shall awake us,
 When calling the dead, in earth's bosom laid low.

7.
Oh! then let us drain, while we may, draughts of pleasure,
 Which from passion, like ours, must unceasingly flow;
Let us pass round the cup of love's bliss, in full

>   measure
>   And quaff the contents, as our nectar below."

The poem begins with a strong and confident expression of the speaker's belief that Caroline loves him. As the next poem in the cycle that I will discuss will show more clearly, it is very important that her declaration does not involve just words--"When I hear you express an affection so warm"--but has physical manifestations as well: "For your lip, would the soul of suspicion disarm,/And your eye beams a ray, which can never deceive." Of the speaker's love for Caroline we are equally convinced; so assured is he, that he refers to it only in a brief phrase, "my belov'd." "To Caroline" seems to be developing into a kind of love poem almost unknown in nineteenth-century literature, especially when compared with poetry of, say, the seventeenth century, in that its subject is not failed or lost love. The situation of the lovers seems to be almost perfect, and we expect the poem to continue in this way, the speaker alternately accepting Caroline's love and asserting his own.

But this is precisely what does not happen. There is a sudden and entirely unexpected change in perspective, once more heralded by "Yet," at the start of the second stanza, that calls the quiet and assured happiness into question. It is as if the restless mind of the speaker cannot remain still for more than a few lines. He introduces two <u>potential</u> threats to their love, and what is remarkable about each is their incredible distance from the lovers' present situation. The first is rather complicated:

> "Yet, still, this fond bosom regrets, whilst adoring,
> That love, like the leaf, must fall into the sear;
> That age will come one, when remembrance deploring
> Contemplates the scenes of her youth, with a tear."

The problem is not simply that time will pass, and then love (like all love seems to be the assumption here) will fade, and "like the leaf, must fall into the sear," though that is part of it. Rather, what disturbs him is the very perfection of his love and his present happiness, the memory of which, when it passes, will bring him pain, as he "contemplates the scenes of (his) youth, with a tear." Somewhat astonishingly, he has altered the perspective to the point where love and pleasure may be perceived as sources of grief and regret.

This shift in perspective is undeniably extreme and odd, and is perceived as such even by the speaker. He responds first by going to great lengths to make sure that his "gloom" is not perceived as doubt or disaffection:

> "Mistake not, sweet sceptic, the cause of emotion,
> No doubt can the mind of your lover invade;
> He worships each look, with such faithful devotion,
> A smile can enchant, no tear can dissuade."

Then he shifts the perspective again--"But"--and the peculiarity of his original idea gives way to a seemingly conventional one. He reminds Caroline that they both will die, and the poem concludes with a vigorous statement of the carpe diem theme.

> "But as death, my belov'd, soon or late shall o'ertake us,
> And our breasts, which alive, with such sympathy glow,

>   Will sleep in the grave, till the blast shall awake us,
>   When calling the dead, in earth's bosom laid low.
>
>   Oh! then let us drain, while we may, draughts of pleasure,
>   Which from passion, like ours, must unceasingly flow;
>   Let us pass round the cup of love's bliss, in full measure,
>   And quaff the contents, as our nectar below."

But this change in point of view is really no less unusual than the previous one. Amazingly, a poem that began with a pronouncement of mutual love turns into "To His Coy Mistress." Nowhere in the poem is there a hint that Caroline needs to be persuaded; in fact, it is her "warm affection" that is expressed at the start, and even at the end the passion is not his, but "ours."

The speaker of this poem is self-conscious to a truly remarkable degree. He seems unable to consider any experience in isolation; even as he is phrasing and hearing declarations of love, his mind is racing forward to the time when they will be spoken no more, either because of disaffection or death. His attitude seems to be a dark and corrosive version of what Eliot termed wit--"a recognition, implicit in the expression of every experience, of other kinds of experience which are possible." But it also resembles those attitudes which Eliot says are sometimes confused with wit. "It is not cynicism, though it has a kind of toughness which may be confused with cynicism by the tender-minded. It is confused with erudition because it belongs to an educated mind, rich in generations of experience; and it is confused with cynicism because it implies a constant inspection and criticism of experience."[8]

One last feature of this poem that should not pass unnoticed is that Caroline is nearly absent from it. The metrical lens is nearly always focused on the speaker's revolving attitudes. Much the same can be said of the second poem in the sequence, which, like the poem I have been discussing, attends to issues of love and language. But the dramatic situation out of which these issues evolve is exactly the opposite.

1.
"You say you love, and yet your eye
  No symptom of that love conveys,
You say you love, yet know not why
  Your cheek no sign of love betrays.

2.
Ah! did that breast with ardour glow,
With me alone it joy could know,
Or feel with me the listless woe,
  Which racks my heart when far from you.

3.
Whene'er we meet, my blushes rise,
  And mantle through my purpled cheek,
But yet no blush to mine replies,
  Nor do those eyes your love bespeak.

4.
Your voice alone declares your flame,
And though so sweet it breathes my name,
Our passions still are not the same,
  Though Love and Rapture still are new.

5.
For e'en your lip seems steep'd in snow,
  And, though so oft it meets my kiss,
It burns with no responsive glow,
  Nor melts, like mine, in dewy bliss.

6.
Ah! what are words to love like mine,
Though uttered by a voice divine,
I still in murmurs must repine,
  And think that love can ne'er be true,

7.

Which meets me with no joyous sign;
  Without a sigh which bids adieu:
How different is that love from mine,
  Which feels such grief when leaving you.

8.

Your image fills my anxious breast,
Till day declines adown the West,
And when, at night, I sink to rest,
  In dreams your fancied form I view.

9.

'Tis then, your breast, no longer cold,
  With equal ardour seems to burn,
While close your arms around me fold,
  Your lips my kiss with warmth return.

10.

Ah! would these joyous moments last!
Vain HOPE! the gay delusion's past;
That voice!--ah! no, 'tis but the blast,
  Which echoes through the neighbouring grove!

11.

But, when <u>awake</u>, your lips I seek,
  And clasp, enraptur'd, all your charms,
So chills the pressure of your cheek,
  I fold a statue in my arms.

12.

If thus, when to my heart embrac'd,
No pleasure in your eyes is trac'd,
You may be prudent, fair, and chaste,
  But ah! my girl, you <u>do not love</u>!"

Basically this poem has been fashioned from a contrast between verbal expressions of love and the physical manifestations which may or may not accompany them, what Byron here calls "symptoms" and "signs."

> "You say you love, and yet your eye
>   No symptom of that love conveys,
> You say you love, yet know not why
>   Your cheek no sign of love betrays."

Just as in the previous poem where Caroline's expression of "affection" was "warm," here she also avers that she loves the speaker; but unlike the earlier situation, there is no correspondence between language and the corporeal demonstrations that in poems of this kind conventionally indicate love. The poem is a small compendium of these totemic emotional eruptions. Unlike Caroline, the speaker "blushes" and "sighs." His breast "burns" with "ardour," his kisses "burn," "glow," and "melt...in dewy bliss." When apart from his beloved his heart is "racked" with "listless woe." Above all he is inarticulate:

> "Ah! what are words to love like mine,
> Though uttered by a voice divine,
> I still in murmurs must repine..."

By contrast, it is Caroline's "voice alone (that) declares (her) flame."

These aspects of the poem place it firmly within a literary tradition of ardent suitors and cold, unfeeling women. And Byron is very much aware that he is working within that tradition. He consciously employs its language, and in the penultimate stanza he alludes to one of its touchstones, Pope's Cloe:

> "But, when awake, your lips I seek,
> And clasp, enraptur'd, all your charms,
> So chills the pressure of your cheek,
> I fold a statue in my arms."

But Caroline's place in this tradition is a curious one. Though we have the speaker's word for it that she is "a statue," a number of lines in the poem suggest that she has been no less active a lover than he. He refers to her declarations of love four times, and at least once in words that suggest heated passion--"And though so sweet it breathes my name." The third stanza suggests that they meet rather often, regularly in fact; how else could he be so certain of their varying responses? If her lip "seems seeped in snow," it still can be found touching his--"And though so <u>oft</u> it meets my kiss" (my italics). And if when he embraces her, he finds her a "statue," there is not a hint in the poem that she has attempted to forbid him these embraces.

It would seem that Caroline is not the problem; and, as earlier, she is more the occasion for the poem than the subject of it. For a poem that purports to be about her, she figures in it conspicuously little. The primary concern, once again, is the speaker's own attitudes. Variations of the first person pronoun appear in these lines twenty-one times. More persuasively, repeatedly in the poem, the speaker makes himself and his responses the measure of all things relating to love:

>"Ah! did that heart with ardour glow,
>With me alone with joy could know,
>Or feel with me the listless woe,
>Which rocks my heart when far from you.
>
>. . .
>
>For e'en your lip seems steep'd in snow,
>And though so oft it meets my kiss,
>It burns with no responsive glow,
>Nor melts with mine in dewy bliss.
>
>. . .
>
>And think that love can ne'er be true,
>Which meets me with no joyous sign;
>Without a sigh which bids adieu:
>How different is that love from mine,
>Which feels such grief when leaving you."

The suggestion is that not only is her love "different" from his, it is really not love at all. As the final line has it, "But ah! my girl, you do not love." That, it would seem, is available only to the speaker.

In both of these poems, Byron is, first of all, attempting to come to terms with the many contradictory passions that have been gathered together into the single word "love," and to dramatize his attitudes toward them. In the earlier poem he considered love from the prospects of old age and death, and from the vantage of the future recalling the past. Here he contrasts two incompatible varieties of love, one that perceives it as of a piece with other comings and goings in the day-to-day world, admitting absences as well as meetings, verbal as well as physical manifestations, and another that regards it as a species apart from the world, the whole, sole, entire reality. To put it in terms of a novel I shall have occasion to return to below, Caroline seeks Edgar Linton, whereas the speaker will have no one but Catherine. It is significant that his contradictions are resolved only when a change in perspective moves the scene (and the poem) away from daily life to the world of dreams:

>"Your image fills my anxious heart,
> Till day declines adown the West,
> And when, at night, I sink to rest,
> In dreams your fancied form I view.
> 'Tis then, your breast, no longer cold,
> With equal ardour seems to burn,
> While close your arms around me fold,
> Your lips my kiss with warmth return.
>
> Ah! would these joyous moments last!
> Vain HOPE! the gay delusion's past;
> That voice!--ah! no, 'tis but the blast,
> Which echoes through the neighboring grave!"

Secondly, in each of these poems, though more elaborately

in this one, Byron is working out his ideas about what
might be designated the relationship between language and
sincerity. This issue dominates all of the poems that
are directly concerned with literature--"To Romance,"
"To a Lady," "The First Kiss of Love," "Stanzas to a Lady,
With the Poems of Camoens," "Lines Written in 'Letters to
an Italian Nun and an English Gentleman'...Answer to the
Foregoing Address'd to Miss Pigot," "Reply to Some Verses
of J.M.B. Pigot, Esq.," and "To the Sighing Strephon"--
and many that are not so expressly about writing. Some
lines from "To a Beautiful Quaker" seem particularly
appropriate to a discussion of "To Caroline":

>"What though we never silence broke,
> Our eyes a sweeter language spoke;
> The tongue in flattering falsehood deals,
> And tells a tale it never feels;
> Deceit, the guilty lips impart,
> And hush the mandates of the heart;
> But soul's interpreters, the eyes,
> Spurn such restraint, and scorn disguise."
> (11.13-20)

As in "To Caroline," language is perceived as a fountainhead
of "flattering falsehoods," "deceit," and "disguise."
More desirable than words are the familiar "symptoms" and
"signs": "the eyes...soul's interpreters." The punctuation
of the first stanza of "To Caroline," when it appeared
in Fugitive Pieces, shaped even stronger suspicions regarding
language. That version has a comma at the end of the third
line, and the stanza concludes, "You say you love, yet know
not why,/Your cheek no sign of love betrays." The distance
between knowing and saying seems unbridgeable; the suggestion
is clearly that she would "know why" *if* the physical "signs"

were present. Finally, both "To a Beautiful Quaker" and the second "To Caroline" point to the superiority of silence--"though we never silence broke/Our eyes a sweet language spoke." As the speaker of "To Caroline" says approvingly of himself, "I still in murmurs must repine," for "what are words to love like mine." And, after all, it is Caroline's "voice," in the guise of the wind, that brings his perfect dream to a close.

In a third poem of the cycle, Byron continues his exploration of love, language and memory from yet another perspective, that of an impossible affair.

> "Think'st thou, I saw thy beauteous eyes,
>   Suffus'd in tears, implore to stay;
> And heard <u>unmov</u>'<u>d</u>, thy plenteous sighs,
>   Which said <u>far</u> more than words can say?
>
> Though keen the grief, <u>thy</u> tears exprest,
>   When love, and hope, <u>lay both</u> o'erthrown,
> Yet still, my girl, <u>this</u> bleeding breast,
>   Throbb'd, with deep sorrow, as <u>thine</u> <u>own</u>.
>
> But, when our cheeks with anguish glow'd,
>   When <u>thy</u> sweet lips were join'd to mine;
> The <u>tears</u>, that from <u>my</u> eye-lids flow'd,
>   Were lost in those which fell from <u>thine</u>.
>
> Thou could'st not feel my burning cheek,
>   <u>Thy</u> gushing tears had quench'd its flame,
> And as thy tongue essay'd to speak,
>   In <u>sighs</u> <u>alone</u> it breath'd my name.
>
> And yet, my girl, we weep in vain,
>   In vain our fate in sighs deplore;
> Remembrance only can remain,
>   But <u>that</u>, will make us weep the more.
>
> Again, thou best belov'd, adieu!
>   Ah! if thou canst o'ercome regret,
> Nor let thy mind past joys review,
>   Our only <u>hope</u> is, to <u>forget</u>."

These lines offer no explanation for why their love cannot be; but the poem that will round out the sequence refers darkly to "foes," "fiends," and "tyrants" who wish to keep them apart. Like the first poem, this one begins with the speaker endeavoring to correct a misunderstanding. He recalls the day he separated from his lover, in order to convince her that she has read the scene incorrectly:

> "Think'st thou, I saw thy beauteous eyes,
>   Suffus'd in tears, implore to stay;
> And heard <u>unmov'd</u>, thy plenteous sighs,
>   Which sa<u>id far</u> more than words can say?"

And, as he indicates in the fourth line, he is no less suspicious of the communicative power of language than the speaker of the poem I have just been considering. But the controversy here--Caroline's inability to perceive that he is as disturbed by their separation as she--has absolutely nothing to do with the unreliability of words; in fact, he is now using words in an effort to clarify his situation and his state of mind. The misunderstanding, in conspicuous contrast with the earlier poem, proceeds from Caroline's failure to understand his non-verbal expressions of emotion, the same "symptoms" and "signs" that previously he so confidently offered as unambiguous and reliable alternatives to language. What once seemed unequivocal, as transparent as writing seen through glass, a direct avenue to the inner life, as it were, has its own perils and hazards. He explains the confusion this way:

> "But, when our cheeks with anguish glow'd,
>   When <u>thy</u> sweet lips were join'd to mine;
> The tea<u>rs</u>, that from <u>my</u> eye-lids flow'd,
>   Were lost in those wh<u>ich</u> fell from <u>thine</u>.
>
> Thou could'st not feel my burning cheek,
>   <u>Thy</u> gushing tears had quench'd its flame,
> And as thy tongue essay'd to speak,

In _sighs_ _alone_ it breath'd my name."
The lines move back and forth from the speaker to Caroline, in a manner that is reminiscent of "Then Peace to thy Spirit." His basic argument is that she was so caught up in her grief that she was unable to notice his, to experience his tears through her own. These lines, far from voicing any mistrust of language, have an almost primitive respect for its powers. Byron's phrasing draws upon the same kinds of poems as the second "To Caroline," as he refers to "my burning cheeks," "Thy gushing tears," and "in sighs alone." But this poem does not accept these as mere figures of speech. Here, "gushing tears" can actually extinguish--"quench"--the flame of a lover's "burning cheek." It is as if various elements of the lachrymose tradition literally cancel each other out.

At this point in the poem, the speaker abandons his explanations, and shifts the perspective from the past to the present and the future. The change is abrupt, and, as before, is introduced with the words, "And yet."

> "And yet, my girl, we weep in vain,
>   In vain our fate in sighs deplore;
> Remembrance only can remain,
>   But _that_, will make us weep the more.
>
> Again, thou best belov'd, adieu!
>   Ah! if thou canst o'ercome regret,
> Nor let thy mind past joys review,
>   Our only _hope_ is, to _forget_."

With these lines, through the sudden revolution in direction, Byron effectively dismantles the poem he has been writing. The speaker's energetic efforts to convince Caroline that he was as deeply moved by their separation as she, which for four stanzas has been the ostensible subject of the poem, turn out to be as "vain" as the lovers' sighs and tears will be in the future. Like them, his emotions at their parting will not make any difference. His explanation does not conclude because he has convinced Caroline--of his success there is not a suggestion; in fact, the turning point occurs immediately after two lines that pointedly and movingly describe her grief, not his: "And as thy tongue essay'd to speak,/In <u>sighs</u> <u>alone</u> it breath'd my name." Rather, in the final stanzas, the whole process of reclaiming the past is called into question, not just remembering "past joys" (which are conspicuously absent here, and are noticed only after the more general interrogation of "remembrance"), but all acts of memory, including the one that has occupied him for sixteen lines. The impulses that were at the heart of the poem's beginning--most simply that something can be learned by recalling the past or that someone can be taught to see an event in a new way, and that these are activities valuable enough to write about--have dissolved. The poem grants to "remembrance" no ameliorating qualities or powers--only, as in the first "To Caroline," painful ones.

> "Remembrance only can remain
> But that will make us weep the more...
> Our only <u>hope</u> is to <u>forget</u>."

The poem that completes the "To Caroline" cycle is the most extreme of the lot. At first glance, it also seems the least dramatic, apparently lacking the shifts in perspective, the sudden, unexpected changes in emphasis, and the tensed sets of contradictory attitudes that make the others so fascinating. Much of it has the appearance of a steady harangue.

> 1.
> "Oh! when shall the grave hide forever my sorrow?
>   Oh! when shall my soul wing her flight from this
>   clay?
> The present is hell! and the coming to-morrow,
>   But brings with new torture, the curse of to-day.
>
> 2.
> From my eye flows no tear, from my lips fall no
>   curses,
>   I blast not the fiends, who have hurl'd me from
>   bliss,
> For poor is the soul which bewailing rehearses
>   Its querulous grief, when in anguish like this--
>
> 3.
> Was my eye, 'stead of tears, with red fury flakes
>   bright'ning,
>   Would my lips breathe a flame, which no stream
>   could assuage,
> On our foes should my glance launch in vengeance its
>   lightning,
>   With transport my tongue give a loose to its rage.
>
> 4.
> But now tears and curses alike unavailing,
>   Would add to the souls of our tyrant's delight;
> Could they view us, our sad separation bewailing,
>   Their merciless hearts would rejoice at the sight.
>
> 5.
> Yet still though we bend with a feign'd resignation,
>   Life beams not for us with one ray that can cheer,
> Love and hope upon earth bring no more consolation,
>   In the grave is our hope, for in life is our fear.
>
> 6.
> Oh! when, my ador'd, in the tomb will they place me,
>   Since in life, love and friendship, for ever are
>   fled,
> If again in the mansion of death I embrace thee,
>   Perhaps they will leave unmolested--the dead."

The poem presents all of its major conflicts as resolved, the last lines expressing the same attitudes and voicing the same desires as the first. It returns to the same dramatic situation as the poem I have just finished reading, an impossible love, but with quite dissimilar feelings and a very different solution to the problem. If there the "only hope is to forget," here it is to die: "In the grave is our hope, for in our life is our fear." Unlike the earlier poem, the speaker makes no gestures toward recalling the lovers' history, either their anguished separation or their "past joys." The emphasis is throughout on the present, which is "hell," and the future, which is only more of the same: "the coming tomorrow,/But brings with new torture the curse of to-day." Though one of the perspectives from which love was viewed in the first poem was also death, the movement here is exactly the opposite. Earlier the thought of dying prompted the speaker to desire more, and more intense, living and loving; now through the turns his life and love have taken, he intensely wishes to die: "Oh! when shall the grave hide forever my sorrow?/Oh! when shall my soul wing its flight from this day?"

In the middle stanzas of the poem, the speaker does consider certain actions that might alter his situation--should he "curse," "blast," or take revenge on those otherwise unspecified "foes" and "tyrants" who have separated the lovers? The third stanza contains a frantic, and indeed, humorous imitation of such heroic activity:

> "Was my eye, 'stead of tears, with red fury flakes bright'ning,
>   Would my lips breathe a flame, which no stream could assuage,
> On our foes should my glance launch in vengeance its lightning,
>   With transport my tongue give a loose to its rage."

But first the ludicrousness of his posture, and then its self-defeating quality ("But now tears and curses alike unavailing./Would add to the souls of our tyrants' delights... Their merciless hearts would rejoice at the sight.") stops him, and he is right back where he started, wishing to die.

The poem seems to have a static quality, the conclusion substantially no different from the start, each line specifying more of the same. And that is precisely right. This is not to say that it is undramatic, in the sense I have been using the word in this essay. The speaker does not act for another, and primary, reason: he has already arrived at a point of view which renders any action unnecessary. If all the conflicts in the poem seem resolved, it is not only because he recognizes and asserts that the lovers cannot be together in this world. Rather, it is because he has already shifted the perspective from this world to one where they can be together. The second "To Caroline" contains a dream in which all of the speaker's doubts and problems drop away, because he has moved on to a realm in which they do not exist. This entire poem functions exactly like that dream, and is a darker, more radical version of it. Its total expression is a dramatic shift in perspective away from an impossible love to a world in which love can thrive. The final lines of the poem find the speaker, like Heathcliff at the conclusion of Wuthering Heights, looking forward to being united with his lover in the grave.

> "Oh! when, my ador'd, in the tomb will they place me,
> Since in life, love and friendship, for ever are fled,
> If again in the mansion of death I embrace thee,
> Perhaps they will leave unmolested--the dead."

The "To Caroline" sequence exemplifies very well Byron's practice of altering the perspective, shifting the point of view, or changing attitude from poem to poem, or within the same poem. Its final effect is the presentation of vigorously inconsistent positions, dispositions, and states of feeling, regarding--among other things--language, memory, dreams, poetry, personal history, time, and love. One of the most suggestive descriptions of the way Byron's voice moves in his early poems can be found, curiously, in Yeats's A Vision. In the mystical scheme of the book, he places Byron at "Phase Nineteen," together with Gabriele d'Annunzio, "a certain actress," and more interestingly, Oscar Wilde. When divested of their occult apparatus, which need not occupy us here, many of his phrases render Byron's irresolute, roving, inconstant voice exactly right. Of the fluctuations, conflicts, and contradictions in the early poetry (and so many other aspects of Byron's life and work--the whole section should be read by anyone interested in him), I know of no more perceptive general account:

> "Unity of Being is no longer possible, for the being is compelled to live in a fragment of itself and to dramatize that fragment...He desires to be strong and stable, but as Unity of Being and self-knowledge are both gone...he passes from emphasis to emphasis...His thought is immensely effective and dramatic, arising always from some immediate situation, a situation found or created by himself, and may have great permanent value as the expression of an

exciting personality. This thought is always
an open attack; or a sudden emphasis, an extravagance...He is tyrannical and capricious,
and his intellect is called 'The Unfaithful,'
because...it will change its ground in a moment and delight in some new emphasis, not
caring whether old and new have consistency."[9]

III

The four poems that are titled "To Caroline" are em-
blematic of the early poetry also in the way that they
embody as well as describe situations that are impossible.
In the same way that the continual shifting of perspectives, attitudes and styles suggests the inadequacies of
any single one, and the limitations of holding on to any
particular style, perspective, or attitude, the four
poems, individually, but more grandly and forcibly as a
sequence, shape a world in which love is nearly impossible.
In these poems love can be maintained only by very energetic and extreme measures. The two poems that involve the
most radical shifts in perspective--to death--are particularly typical of the early work. For not only are the
shifts in perspective that I have been describing perhaps
the preeminent characteristic of the early poems; more often
than not, that shift involves some reference to death.
Some other representative poems of this kind are "Epitaph
on a Friend," "To M.S.G.," "Stanzas" ("I would I were a careless child"), "To Mary," "To the Earl of Clare," "Lines
Written Beneath an Elm in the Churchyard of Harrow on the
Hill," "The First Kiss of Love," "The Tear," and "Childish
Recollections." In each of these poems, the speakers are

reminded, often abruptly, of their own deaths, or actively wish that they might die.

"Childish Recollections"[10] is the controlling poem of all the early work, embracing to one degree or another the entire range of its tones and attitudes, much as a single dot from a hologram contains all of the information on the whole photographic plate. The poem begins with the speaker sick and dying, seeking ways to alleviate his affliction.

"When slow Disease with all her host of Pains,
Chills the warm tide, which flows along the veins;
When Health affrighted spreads her rosy wing,
And flies with every changing gale of spring;
Not to the aching frame alone confin'd,
Unyielding pangs assail the drooping mind:
What grisly forms, the spectre train of woe!
Bid shuddering Nature shrink beneath the blow,
With Resignation wage relentless strife,
While Hope retires appall'd, and clings to life.
Yet less the pang, when, through the tedious hour,
Remembrance sheds around her genial power,
Calls back the vanish'd days to rapture given,
When Love was bliss, and Beauty form'd our heaven;
Or dear to youth, portrays each childish scene,
Those fairy bowers, where all in turn have been.
As when, through clouds that pour the summer storm,
The orb of day unveils his distant form,
Gilds with faint beams the chrystal dews of rain,
And dimly twinkles o'er the watery plain;
Thus, while the future dark and cheerless gleams,
The Sun of Memory, glowing through my dreams,
Though sunk the radiance of his former blaze,
To scenes far distant points his paler rays,
Still rules my senses with unbounded sway,
The past confounding with the present day.

Oft does my heart indulge the rising thought,
Which still recurs, unlook'd for, and unsought;
My soul to Fancy's fond suggestion yields,
And roams romantic o'er her airy fields;
Scenes of my youth, develop'd, croud to view,
To which I long have bade a last adieu!
Seats of delight, inspiring youthful themes;
Friends lost to me, for aye, except in dreams;
Some, who in marble prematurely sleep,
Whose forms I now remember, but to weep;
Some, who yet urge the same scholastic course

>   Of early science, future fame the source:
>   Who, still contending in the studious race,
>   In quick rotation, fill the senior place!
>   These, with a thousand visions, now unite,
>   To dazzle, though they please, my aching sight."
>   (ll.1-42)

The speaker is ill physically, to be sure, but he is also distressed mentally. As disease takes over his body, along with the attendant "chills," and "aches," he begins to experience terrifying hallucinations: "Unyielding pangs assail the drooping mind:/What grisly forms, the spectre train of woe!" The present version does not specify exactly what "grisly forms" make up "the spectre train"; but in the earlier one, the suggestion is that he is being visited by uninvited ("in vain I check the maddening thought,/It still recurs, unlook'd for, and unsought.") guests from his past, and that his "woe" largely is due to a contrast between what he is now, and what he once was:

>   "Hence! thou unvarying song, of varied loves,
>   While youth commends, maturer age reproves;
>   Which every rhyming bard repeats by rote,
>   By thousands echo'd to the self same note;
>
>   Tir'd of the dull, unceasing, copious strain,
>   My soul is panting to be free again.
>   Farewell! ye nymphs, propitious to my verse,
>   Some other Damon, will your charms rehearse;
>   Some other paint his pangs, in hope of bliss,
>   Or dwell in rapture, on your nectar'd kiss,
>   Those beauties grateful, to my ardent sight,
>   No more entrance my senses in delight.
>   Those bosoms, form'd of animated snow,
>   Alike are tasteless and unfeeling now.
>   These, to some happier lover, I resign;
>   The memory of those joys alone is mine.
>   Censure no more shall brand my humble name,
>   The child of passion, and the fool of fame.
>   Weary of love, of life, devour'd with spleen,
>   I rest, a perfect Timon, not nineteen;

> World! I renounce thee! all my hope's o'ercast;
> One sigh I give thee, but that sigh's the last,
> Friends, foes, and females, now alike, adieu!
> Would I could add, remembrance of you, too.
> Yet, though the future, dark and cheerless gleams,
> The curse of memory, hovering in my dreams,
> Depicts, with glowing pencil, all those years,
> Ere yet, my cup, empoison'd flow'd, with tears,
> Still rules my senses with tyrannic sway,
> The past confounding with the present day.
>
> Alas! in vain I check the maddening thought,
> It still recurs, unlook'd for, and unsought;"
>   POVO (ll.1-28)

The later version also emphasizes the differences between past and present, though not so radically. The "days" when "Love was bliss, and Beauty form'd our heaven," have "vanish'd." In the second verse paragraph, he writes of, "Friends lost to me, for aye, except in dreams;/Some who in marble prematurely sleep,/whose forms I now remember, but to weep." And he deprecates the joys of his early days a bit, even as he delights in them--he speaks of "<u>fairy</u> bowers," "<u>indulg(ing)</u> the rising thought," "yielding to Fancy's <u>fond</u> suggestion," and roaming "<u>romantic</u>," as if to censure them as foolish and puerile (my italics; also, Byron often uses "fond" and "romantic" in their negative sense, one to specify "folly," the other "extravagance").

But much more significantly, the present version moves in precisely the opposite direction from the earlier one. There, it was his poetry that was infirm, as it were ("Tir'd of the dull, unceasing, copious strain..."), and "memory" was regarded as a "curse." However, now it is to poetry and to "remembrance" that the speaker turns for relief, and for diminishment of his pain:

> "Yet less the pang, when, through the tedious hour,
> Remembrance sheds around her genial power...
> Thus, while the future dark and cheerless gleams,
> The Sun of Memory, glowing through my dreams,
> Though sunk, the radiance of his former blaze,
> To scenes far distant points his paler rays,
> Still rules my senses with unbounded sway,
> The past confounding with the present day."
> (ll.11-12; 21-26)

"Childish Recollections," as its most recent editor has pointed out, is indebted to the tradition of eighteenth-century retrospective poetry, particularly Henry Kirke White's "Childhood."[11] But it is also closely allied, in impulse at least, with poems like Wordsworth's "Tintern Abbey," in that it describes a poet's return to an earlier source of strength, hoping that he will be revivified through fresh contact with its "genial power." It should also quickly be noted that in no other way than this, admittedly important one, is this poem at all Wordsworthian.

In "Childish Recollections," then, the speaker seeks to return to the scenes of his past, not just for purposes of nostalgia, but to dispel, if only briefly, the "unyielding pangs" and "grisly forms" that afflict him. Each of the first two paragraphs ends with an assertion that he has achieved his purposes--in the first, "Still rules my senses with unbounded sway,/The past confounding with the present day."; and in the second, "These, with a thousand visions, now unite,/To dazzle, though they please, my aching sight." But these lines are the only places in "Childish Recollections" where past and present merge in an effective manner, or where the past is a source of nourishment and strength. What the poem goes on poignantly to demonstrate is his inability to reclaim the past, and the painful differences between his past and present. The poem that follows is much more like what one would have expected from the cancelled lines from Poems on Various Occasions that I quoted above.

In the third paragraph, he turns, as most of his retrospective poems do, to "Ida" (Harrow):

> "IDA! blest spot, where Science holds her reign,
> How joyous, once, I join'd thy youthful train;
> Bright, in idea, gleams thy lofty spire,
> Again, I mingle with thy playful quire;
> Our tricks of mischief, every childish game,
> Unchang'd by time or distance, seem the same;
> Through winding paths, along the glade I trace,
> The social smile of ev'ry welcome face,
> My wonted haunts, my scenes of joy or woe,
> Each early boyish friend, or youthful foe,
> Our feuds dissolv'd, but not my friendship past,
> I bless the former, and forgive the last.
> Hours of my youth, when nurtur'd in my breast,
> To Love a stranger, Friendship made me blest;"
> (ll.43-56)

He begins by recalling his beloved school, its grounds, his friends, and their games and pranks, with much delight. First he remembers fondly ("How joyous once..."), and then, in a leap of the imagination, rejoins ("Again, I mingle...") his youthful scenes and days. He asserts that Ida, his friends, and himself are "Unchang'd by time or distance." Yet, certain words and phrases begin to eat away at the identification he is attempting to establish. Ida's spire gleams bright only "in idea." His friends, the school, and himself only "seem the same." He starts to recollect people and events that were not so pleasant, "Each...youthful foe...Our feuds dissolv'd" and as he forgives them, in retrospect, he is already taking the first step toward distancing himself from the scene. Finally, the lines about love, friendship, and youth lead him into a much longer tirade that establishes just how much "time" and "distance" have changed them all.

> "Friendship, the dear peculiar bond of youth,
> When every artless bosom throbs with truth;
> Untaught by worldly wisdom how to feign,
> And check each impulse with prudential rein;
> When, all we feel, our honest souls disclose,
> In love to friends, in open hate to foes;
> No varnish'd tales the lips of youth repeat,
> No dear bought knowledge purchas'd by deceit;
> Hypocrisy, the gift of lengthen'd years,
> Matur'd by age, the garb of Prudence wears;
> When, now the Boy is ripen'd into Man,
> His careful Sire chalks forth some wary plan;
> Instructs his Son from Candour's path to shrink,
> Smoothly to speak, and cautiously to think;
> Still to assent, and never to deny,
> A patron's praise can well reward the lie;
> And who, when Fortune's warning voice is heard,
> Would lose his opening prospects for a word?
> Although, against that word, his heart rebel,
> And Truth, indignant, all his bosom swell."

Quite properly, given the kind of poem he has announced, and his reasons for writing it, he suddenly brings this to a stop, castigates himself, and begins the next paragraph by saying,

> "Away with themes like this, not mine the task,
> From flattering fiends to tear the hateful mask;
> Let keener banks delight in Satire's sting,
> My fancy soars not on Detraction's wing;"
> (ll.77-80)

With great energy, he proclaims the inappropriateness of the lines he has just set down. Curiously, he does not cancel them, and replace them with others more in keeping with the tone he struck at the outset of the paragraph. Even more oddly, he goes on to record another occasion when he took "delight in Satire's sting." And not only does he recall the incident, he paraphrases the earlier satire at some length:

> "Once, and but once, she aim'd a deadly blow,
> To hurl Defiance on a secret Foe;
> But, when that Foe, from feeling or from shame,
> The cause unknown, yet still to me the same,
> Warn'd by some friendly hint, perchance, retir'd,
> With this submission, all her rage expir'd.
> From dreaded pangs that feeble Foe to save,
> She hush'd her young resentment, and forgave:
> Or, if my Muse a Pedant's portrait drew,
> Pomposus' virtues are but known to few;
> I never fear'd the young usurper's nod,
> And he who wields, must, sometimes, feel the rod.
> If since, on Granta's failings, known to all,
> Who share the converse of a college hall,
> She sometimes trifled in a lighter strain,
> 'Tis past, and thus she will not sin again.
> Soon must her early song forever cease,
> And, all may rail, when I shall rest in peace."
> (ll.81-98)

The paragraph ends as it began, with the speaker trumpeting that he will not do again what he has just done. And besides, he adds, all may direct satires against him after he has passed away. This reference to his impending death recalls the opening lines of the poem, and reminds him of the theme he announced there, and which has been avoided so resolutely thus far. In the next paragraph, he finally inaugurates his recollections:

> "Here, first remembered be the joyous band,
> Who hail'd me chief, obedient to command;
> Who join'd with me, in every boyish sport,
> Their first adviser, and their last resort."
> (ll.99-102)

"First remembered" is a kind of pun. Not only is "the joyous band" of friends what he most fondly remembers from his past, but these lines are first real reminiscences of the sort he proclaimed at the start of the poem--"the vanished days to rapture given." But, incredibly, he sustains them for only four lines. The "joyous band" does not reenter the poem until 1.243, and he takes up again his attack on "Pomposus," shifting gears only to lament the loss of his predecessor, "Probus":

> "Nor shrunk before the upstart pedant's frown,
> Or all the sable glories of his gown;
> Who, thus transplanted from his father's school,
> Unfit to govern, ignorant of rule,
> Succeeded him, whom all unite to praise,
> The dear preceptor of my early days;
> Probus, the pride of science, and the boast,
> To IDA, now, alas! for ever lost.
> With him, for years, we search'd the classic page,
> And fear'd the Master, though we lov'd the Sage;
> Retir'd at last, his small, yet peaceful seat,
> From learning's labour is the blest retreat.
> Pomposus fills his magisterial chair;
> Pomposus governs,--but my Muse forbear:
> Contempt, in silence, be the pedant's lot,
> His name and precepts be alike forgot;
> No more his mention shall my verse degrade,
> To him my tribute is already paid."
> (ll.103-120)

This conclusion is all too familiar by now. For the third time he has dismissed certain subjects as unfit for his poem even as he is considering them. We are now 120 lines into "Childish Recollections," and barely more than a dozen have had anything to do with "Remembrance shed(ding) around her genial power." Each time he attempts to return to a scene of this nature, and recapture it in his verse, another recollection--at cross-purposes with it--enters his mind bringing the first memory to an abrupt halt. Just as in the shorter works I discussed earlier, other perspectives are introduced into the paragraphs of this poem, altering and disturbing the original one, in this case, his search for "genial power."

Though "Pomposus" does make one more brief appearance in the poem, this is really the last of the satirical paragraphs. In the next one, it is almost as if "Childish Recollections" has been begun all over again; and the speaker embarks upon what appears to be a long, uninhibited stretch of sustained remembrance.

>"High, thro' those elms with hoary branches
>   crown'd,
>Fair IDA'S bower adorns the landscape round;
>There Science from her favor'd seat surveys
>The vale, where rural Nature claims her praise;
>To her awhile resigns her youthful train,
>Who move in joy, and dance along the plain,
>In scatter'd groupes each favoured haunt pursue,
>Repeat old pastimes, and discover new;
>Flush'd with his rays, beneath the moon-tide Sun,
>In rival bands, between the wickets run,
>Drive o'er the sward the ball with active force,
>Or chase with nimble feet its rapid course.
>But these with slower steps direct their way,
>Where Brent's cool waves in limpid currents stray;
>While yonder few search out some green retreat;
>And arbours shade them from the summer heat;
>Others, again, a pert, and lively crew,
>Some rough, and thoughtless stranger plac'd in view,
>With frolic quaint, their antic jests expose
>And tease the grumbling rustic as he goes;
>Nor rest with this, but many a passing fray,
>Tradition treasures for a future day;
>'Twas here the gather'd swains for vengeance fought,
>And here we earn'd the conquest dearly bought,
>Here have we fled before superior might,
>And here renew'd the wild tumultuous fight.'
>While thus our souls with early passions swell,
>In lingering tones resounds the distant bell;
>Th' allotted hour of daily sport is o'er,
>And Learning beckons from her temple's door.
>No splendid tablets grace her simple hall,
>But ruder records fill the dusky wall;
>There, deeply carv'd, behold! each Tyro's name
>Secures its owner's academic fame;
>Here, mingling view the names of Sire and Son,
>The one long grav'd, the other just begun,
>These shall survive alike when Son and Sire,
>Beneath one common stroke of fate expire,
>Perhaps, their last memorial these alone,
>Denied, in Death, a monumental stone,
>Whilst to the gale, in mournful cadence wave,
>The sighing weeds, that hide their nameless grave.
>And, here, my name and many an early friend's
>Along the wall in lengthened line extends,
>Though, still, our deeds amuse the youthful race,

>   Who tread our steps, and fill our former place,
>   Who young obeyed their lords in silent awe,
>   Whose nod commanded, and whose voice was law;
>   And now, in turn, possess the reins of power,
>   To rule the little Tyrants of an hour;
>   Though sometimes, with the Tales of ancient day,
>   They pass the dreary Winter's eve away;
>   'And, thus, our former rulers stemm'd the tide,
>   And, thus, they dealt the combat, side by side;
>   Just in this place, the mouldering walls they scaled,
>   Nor bolts, nor bars, against their strength availed;
>   Here, Probus came, the rising fray to quell,
>   And, here, he faultered forth his last farewell,
>   And, here, one night, abroad they dared to roam,
>   While bold Pomposus bravely staid at home.'
>   While thus they speak, the hour must soon arrive,
>   When names of these, like ours, alone survive;
>   Yet a few years, one general wreck will whelm
>   The faint remembrance of our fairy realm."
>   (ll.121-184)

The first section of this paragraph offers an affecting, if somewhat conventional, account of the various activities that composed a single day at "Ida." Though his insistence on keeping all of the disparate elements of the scene before us at the same time ("These...Where...In scatter'd groups... But there...While yonder few...," etc.) suggests that he has late eighteenth-century landscape painting in mind, he seems not at all distanced from the events he is describing. In this initial description he seems to be accomplishing what he only thought he achieved earlier--all is "Unchang'd by time or distance."

Three times in the course of the lines that follow this recital of "Ida's" exterior pleasures, he makes claims for the permanence of the events that he is recalling; first, when he writes of "many a passing fray,/Tradition treasures for a future day"; then, "There, deeply carv'd, behold! each Tyro's name/Secures its owner's academic fame...

These shall survive alike when Son and Sire,/Beneath one
common stroke of fate expire..."; and, lastly, in the passage beginning, "Though, still, our deeds amuse the youthful race...," when he imagines future generations of "Ida's"
students recalling the speaker and his friends. What is
curious about each of these claims for perpetuity is the
way that it tends to disrupt the progress of the paragraph,
drawing attention to the strains behind the seemingly
casual and easy reminiscences, and upsetting the air of
uncomplicated immediacy that had been so artfully established in the absorbing genre painting that began it. The
lines that surround these three claims are not so much recollections as they are skewed and self-conscious versions of
them, or vacant, artificial substitutes. Consider the most
powerful assertion of permanence, the second:

> "No splendid tablets grace her simple hall,
> But ruder records fill the dusky wall;
> There, deeply carv'd, behold! each Tyro's name
> Secures its owner's academic fame;
> Here, mingling view the names of Sire and Son,
> The one long grav'd, the other just begun,
> These shall survive alike when Son and Sire,
> Beneath one common stroke of fate expire,
> Perhaps, their last memorial these alone,
> Denied, in Death, a monumental stone,
> Whilst to the gale, in mournful cadence wave,
> The sighing weeds, that hide their nameless grave."
> (11.151-162)

He refers only to a wooden roster on a wall, and involves
the engaged, active memory not at all. It bears the same
relationship to personal recollection that owning an encyclopedia does to a profession of scholarship. The first
is the most disruptive of the graceful and effortless
melding of past and present that the speaker had disarmingly

effected:

> "Nor rest with this, but many a passing fray,
> Tradition treasures for a future day;
> 'Twas here the gather'd swains for vengeance fought,
> And here we earn'd the conquest dearly bought,
> Here have we fled before superior might,
> And here renew'd the wild tumultuous fight."
> (ll.141-146)

What he is recalling here, no less, are occasions in the past when he anticipated recalling the very moment he is remembering now. There is a pathos in these lines--a young man already prescient of his future need of a nourishing past--but pathos is utterly at odds with the mood of vital involvement that the speaker is endeavoring to promote here, as is the extreme self-consciousness, which adds a note of desperation, and perhaps of falseness, to his present effort to secure a sustaining past. Finally, by the time he reaches the third assertion, the claims for permanence are only apparently there, and with quiet but still powerful irony, he exposes as artificial and forced the scene he had so skillfully sketched in the opening lines of the paragraph. For the final claim of immortality is, in fact, no claim at all:

> "Though, still, our deeds amuse the youthful race,
> Who tread our steps, and fill our former place,
> Who young obeyed their lords in silent awe,
> Whose nod commanded, and whose voice was law:
> And now, in turn, possess the reins of power,
> To rule the little Tyrants of an hour;
> Though sometimes, with the Tales of ancient day,
> They pass the dreary Winter's eve away:
> 'And, thus, they dealt the combat, side by side;
> Just in this place, the mouldering walls they scaled,
> Nor bolts, nor bars, against their strength availed;
> Here, Probus came, the rising fray to quell,
> And, here, he faultered forth his last farewell,
> And, here, one night, abroad they dared to roam,
> While bold Pompous bravely staid at home.'"
> (ll.165-180)

His past life becomes a species of schoolboy folk literature. In Shakespeare's play, to which these lines delicately make reference, "A sad tale's best for winter." And the story the students repeat, though concerned with youthful power and victories over teachers and masters, is sad too, but they are too young to know it. Only the speaker apprehends just how pathetic these reminiscences are:

> "While thus they speak, the hour must soon arrive,
> When names of these, like ours, alone survive;
> Yet a few years, one general wreck will whelm
> The faint remembrance of our fairy realm."
> (ll.181-184)

In the opening lines of the poem, he expressed his desire to make the "fairy bowers" of his youth live again, so that, in his sickness, the memory might refresh and animate him. Here, the "fairy realm" comes to a cheerless, violent end, the whole experience accrueing bitterness from its very casualness, and the fact that no one really notices-- "While thus they speak..."

After this point in "Childish Recollections," although we are not quite halfway through it, the speaker abandons his search for a nourishing past and, for the most part, avoids sustained recollection as well. What occupies him for the rest of the poem are a series of often contradictory meditations on memory, on his reasons for wishing to reconsider the past, and on the differences between his past and the kind of life he leads now. For instance, in the next paragraph he writes, in direct opposition to what we have been reading, that since parting with Ida and his young friends, he has consciously lived in a fashion designed to make him "forget" them:

> "Dear honest race, though now we meet no more,
> One last, long look on what we were before;
> Our first kind greetings, and our last adieu!
> Drew tears from eyes unus'd to weep with you;
> Through splendid circles, Fashion's gaudy world,
> Where Folly's glaring standard waves unfurl'd,
> I plung'd to drown in noise my fond regret,
> And all I sought or hop'd, was to forget:
> (ll.185-192)

These lines very much anticipate the opening stanzas of <u>Childe Harold</u>. What is especially poignant about them is their careful blending of his actual farewell to his friends and the one he has just taken in the poem; he shed tears then, and he is weeping now, as he writes his "One, last long look on what we were before." This time the forceful self-consciousness--remembering a moment when he was trying to forget--adds to the effect he is creating, and is of a piece with the pain he is describing. But his "plunge" into the fashionable world, for all its diverting "noise" and "splendor," would not let him forget "what we were before." The paragraph continues:

> "Vain wish! if, chance, some well remember'd face,
> Some old companion of my early race,
> Advanc'd to claim his friend with honest joy,
> My eyes, my heart proclaim'd me still a boy;
> The glittering scene, the fluttering groupes around,
> Were quite forgotten, when my friend was found;
> The smiles of Beauty, (for, alas! I've known
> What 'tis to bend before Love's mighty throne;)
> The smiles of Beauty, though those smiles were dear,
> Could hardly charm me, when that friend was near;
> My thoughts bewilder'd in the fond surprise,
> The woods of Ida danc'd before my eyes;
> I saw the sprightly wand'rers pour along,
> I saw, and join'd again the joyous throng;
> Panting again, I trac'd her lofty grove,
> And Friendship's feelings triumph'd over Love."
> (ll.193-209)

The speaker's language--"My eyes, my heart proclaim'd me still a boy," and, especially, the lively description of "Ida," "I saw and joined again the joyous throng;/Panting again, I trac'd her lofty grove..."--seems to suggest that in his chance encounter with "Some old companion of my early race," he accomplished what he has been unable to do in "Childish Recollections." But the two situations are really not at all alike. At the outset of the poem, he hoped that reviewing the past would bring him strength for the present. Here he records a moment when events conspired to create the illusion that he was still living in the past, and that time had simply stopped. The present picture is of a man who wishes to submerge the complexities and difficulties of his life in nostalgia; but it was sustenance, not nostalgia, that he was seeking earlier. For whatever his eyes and heart proclaim, he is not "still a boy."

In the next paragraph he asks himself why he should be so interested in the past, implicitly questioning the poem he is writing: "Yet, why should I alone with such delight/Retrace the circuit of my former flight?" The reasons he offers all point to persistent solitude, both early in his life and recently (in essence, both before and after he was at "Ida"), and a pervasive sense of isolation. He speaks of the early death of his father, and his lack of a sister or a brother. He does not mention his mother at all--curiously, since she, and his sister Augusta as well, are so prominent in the letters of this period. Along the way, he portrays Ida as a lost paradise:

> "Ah! sure some stronger impulse vibrates here,
> Which whispers friendship will be doubly dear
> To one, who thus for kindred hearts must roam,
> And seek abroad, the love denied at home:
> Those hearts, dear Ida, have I found in thee,
> A home, a world, a paradise to me."
> (11.213-218)

Youth, or more often childhood, is a paradise from which the poet has been banished in many of the early poems, most persuasively in "Stanzas" ("I would I were a careless child"), and "Song" ("When I rov'd a young Highlander, o'er the dark heath"). Robert F. Gleckner has written a fine book on the place of this theme in all of Byron's poetry, <u>Byron and the Ruins of Paradise</u>.[12] In a direct sense, the opening lines of "Childish Recollections" mark it as an attempt to forge a personal <u>Paradise Regained</u>, though the poem that he actually wrote has <u>Paradise Lost</u> much more forcibly behind it.

In the middle of his description of his solitary and lonely childhood he records a dream that clarifies and amplifies his sense of loss and forfeiture:

> "Oft, in the progress of some fleeting dream,
> Fraternal smiles, collected round me seem,
> While still the visions to my heart are prest,
> The voice of Love will murmur in my rest;
> I hear, I wake, and in the sound rejoice,
> I hear again--but ah! no Brother's voice."
> (11.229-234)

This dream resembles the one in the second "To Caroline," and serves the same function. It marks a shift in perspective to a world where, if only momentarily, his problems no longer oppress him. In the present poem, it serves as a temporary shelter, much like the nostalgia he took refuge in earlier. He then goes on to characterize his current situation:

> "A Hermit, midst of crowds, I fain must stray
> Alone, though thousand pilgrims fill the way;
> While these a thousand kindred wreaths entwine,
> I cannot call one single blossom mine:
> What then remains? in solitude to groan,
> To mix in friendship, or to sigh alone?
> Thus, must I cling to some endearing hand,
> And none more dear, than Ida's social band."
> (ll.235-242)

Once again, the language the speaker brings to his life looks forward to Childe Harold. His image of himself, and of the choices available to him are radical and desperate; but no less so is the solution he reaches for: "Thus, must I cling to some endearing hand,/And none more dear, than Ida's social band." It is hard to say how this differs from "sigh(ing) alone." The hands that he so recklessly, and as a last resort, "clings" to are in no sense "actual" hands--or, more properly, they are not actually present for him. They belong to the past, and once more he seeks a haven in nostalgia.

The five celebrated portraits that follow (ll.243-340) establish this even more clearly. Each rehearses a few anecdotes from their days together at "Ida;" each carries exuberant praise for the particular friend; and in each there is a prediction of future greatness. But nowhere is there any sense that "Alonzo" or "Davus" or "Lycus" or "Euryalus" or "Cleon" participate in the speaker's current life. Each portrait is firmly rooted in the past, and the gulf between past and present seems absolute. They are not at all "recollections" in the sense that he invoked at the start of the poem, when he wrote of "The Sun of Memory, glowing through my dreams...The past confounding with the present day." Their total and final effect is almost precisely the converse. They demonstrate how unconfounded and distant are his past and present days. It is almost as if when he writes about each friend, he is cataloguing him, and filing him away, so little connection does each have with the life he is now leading. They read almost like testimonials, or even eulogies. This last comparison is not at all recondite, as in the lines that immediately follow the final portrait, he describes what he has been doing as "Remembrance...Drooping...o'er pensive Fancy's urn."

> "Oh! Friends regretted, Scenes for each dear,
> Remembrance hails you, with her warmest tear!
> Drooping, she bends, o'er pensive Fancy's urn,
> To trace the hours, which never can return,
> Yet, with the retrospection loves to dwell,
> And soothe the sorrows of her last farewell!
> Yet, greets the triumph, of my boyish mind..."
> (11.341-347)

Like the portraits, these lines emphasize distance--"To trace the hours, which never can return." "Regretted" is a word which is applied to reminiscences in at least six other poems from this period. Here, as throughout "Childish Recollections," the speaker debates with himself the value of recalling the past ("Friends regretted, Scenes forever dear...Yet...Yet..."). Even at the end of this long poem he is not entirely sure that he wishes to be writing it. More and more the subject turns to poetry. In the lines that immediately succeed the ones I just quoted, he combines homage to "Probus" with a discussion of his verse, early and recent:

> "As infant laurels round my head were twin'd:
> When Probus' praise repaid my lyric song,
> Or plac'd me higher in the studious throng;
> Or, when my first harangue receiv'd applause,
> His sage instruction the primaeval cause,
> What gratitude, to him, my soul possest,
> While hope of dawning honours fill'd my breast.
> For all my humble fame, to him alone,
> The praise is due, who made that fame my own.
> Oh! could I soar above these feeble lays,
> These young effusions of my early days,
> To him my Muse her noblest strain would give,
> The song might perish, but the theme must live;
> Yet, why for him the needless verse essay?
> His honour'd name requires no vain display;
> By every son of grateful Ida blest,
> It finds an echo in each youthful breast;
> A fame beyond the glories of the proud,
> Or all the plaudits of the venal crowd.

Only a few lines away from ending the poem, he pauses to question his ability to write it. Similarly, his sense of what the poem is really about becomes unfocused. Why, in a poem so anxious about coming to terms with the past, reclaiming it, and fashioning it into a sustaining, nourishing force, should he consciously leave something out, because there are other ways of preserving it--ways that he has already discredited? "Yet, why for him the needless verse essay?" And the poem has two endings, one personal, the other addressed to all men, that sound equally convincing and conclusive.

These confusions and difficulties correspond with the uncertainties and contradictions out of which the poem has been created. When at the start, the speaker wrote, "Yet less the pang, when, through the tedious hour,/Remembrance sheds around her genial power," his desire was similar to Wordsworth's in "My Heart Leaps Up":

> "And I could wish my days to be
> Bound each to each by natural piety."

"Childish Recollections," though little concerned with "natural piety," is the record of his failure to bind his days together "each to each." What dominates the ending of the poem is, first of all, a sense of bitterness about the present. Then, he is ambivalent about the whole process of locating a restorative power in the past. And lastly, he is captivated by nostalgia. As he writes in the penultimate paragraph of the poem,

> "IDA, not yet exhausted is the theme,
> Nor clos'd the progress of my youthful dream;
> How many a friend deserves the grateful strain!
> What scenes of childhood still unsung remain!
> Yet let me hush this echo of the past,
> This parting song, the dearest and the last;
> And brood in secret o'er those hours of joy,
> To me a silent, and a sweet employ,
> While future hope and fear alike unknown,
> I think with pleasure on the past alone;
> Yes, to the past alone, my heart confine,
> And chase the phantom of what once was mine."

In the earlier version of "Childish Recollections," there is less emphasis on nostalgia, but greater bitterness, and a fiercer ambivalence. In a passage which I cited earlier, what is here "The Sun of Memory" was originally "The curse of memory." And he renounces nearly every aspect of the poem's apparatus, but especially "remembrance," which is described in language that makes death seem more deserving of preference. Some of these lines are worth reading again, this time more securely established in their context.

> "Ah! vain endeavour, in this childish strain,
> To soothe the woes, of which I thus complain;
> What can avail this fruitless loss of time,

> To measure sorrow, in a jingling rhyme!
> No social solace, from a friend, is near,
> And heartless strangers drop no feeling tear.
> I seek not joy, in woman's sparkling eye,
> The smiles of beauty cannot check the sigh.
> Adieu! thou world! thy pleasure's still a dream
> Thy virtue, but a visionary theme;
> Thy years of vice, on years of folly roll,
> 'Till grinning death assigns the destin'd goal;
> Where all are hastening to the dread abode,
> To meet the judgement of a righteous God;
> Mix'd in the concourse of the thoughtless throng,
> A mourner, 'midst of mirth, I glide along;
> A wretched, isolated, gloomy thing,
> Curst by reflection's deep corroding sting:
>
> . . .
>
> Not crimes I mourn, but happiness gone by.
> Thus, crawling on with many a reptile vile,
> My heart is bitter, though my cheek may smile;
> No more, with former bliss, my breast is glad,
> Hope yields to anguish, and my soul is sad:
> From fond regret, no future joy can save,
> Remembrance slumbers only in the grave."
>   POVO (11.361-378; 406-412)

The poem was probably improved with the cancellation of this section. It perhaps renders too plainly and explicitly the sense of final and total loss that the later version much more quietly imparts. But its bitter cynicism and withering negativity are perhaps more in the spirit of the epigraph that graced the poem both times Byron printed it: "I cannot but remember such things were,/And were most dear to me." Slightly misquoted, they are Macduff's words upon hearing that his wife and children have been murdered.

IV

If "Childish Recollections" is the controlling poem in these early collections, then "remembrance" is the commanding subject. Not all of the poems are as negative, or even as ambivalent, about the past. In fact, in the poem which Byron placed first in each of three editions that he both authorized and supervised, "On Leaving Newstead Abbey," tones and attitudes are disclosed that, perhaps, could not be imagined from the lines I have just been discussing. It precedes "Childish Recollections" by three years:

> "Thro' thy battlements, Newstead, the hollow winds whistle,
> Thou, the hall of my fathers, art gone to decay;
> In thy once smiling garden, the hemlock and thistle
> Have choak'd up the rose, which late bloom'd in the way.
>
> Of the mail-cover'd Barons, who proudly to battle,
> Led their vassals from Europe to Palestine's plain,
> The escutcheon and shield, which with every blast rattle,
> Are the only sad vestiges now that remain.
>
> No more doth old Robert, with harp-stringing numbers,
> Raise a flame in the breast, for the war-laurel'd wreath;
> Near Askalon's towers, John of Horistan slumbers,
> Unnerv'd is the hand of his minstrel, by death.
>
> Paul and Hubert too sleep, in the valley of Cressy,
> For the safety of Edward and England they fell;
> My fathers! the tears of your country redress ye;
> How you fought! how you died! still her annals can tell.
>
> On Marston, with Rupert, 'gainst traitors contending,
> Four brothers enrich'd, with their blood, the bleak field;
> For the rights of a monarch, their country defending,
> Till death their attachment to royalty seal'd.
>
> Shades of heroes, farewell! your descendant, departing
> From the seat of his ancestors, bids you, adieu!
> Abroad, or at home, your remembrance imparting
> New courage, he'll think upon glory, and you.
>
> Though a tear dim his eye, at this sad separation,
> 'Tis nature, not fear, that excites his regret;
> Far distant he goes, with the same emulation,
> The fame of his fathers he ne'er can forget.
>
> That fame, and that memory, still will he cherish,
> He vows, that he ne'er will disgrace your renown;

> Like you will he live, or like you will he perish;
> When decay'd, may he mingle his dust with your own."

This is one of the most serious and earnest pieces that Byron ever wrote; it is also, perhaps for that reason, one of the least satisfying. The poems that he did deem worthy of publishing in <u>Fugitive Pieces</u> rarely contain as many graceless and plodding lines as this. But what is significant about "On Leaving Newstead Abbey" is the speaker's confidence in the power of the past to animate the present and provide strength for the future. The poem is an ardent expression of faith. It begins with a description of immense "decay"; but nowhere in the poem is this a source of regret. On the contrary, the "decay" of Newstead Abbey is more something to be relished--it is a sign that greatness has resided there for a long time. In the course of the poem, the speaker expresses his uncomplicated admiration of the actions of his ancestors, and an equally uncomplicated trust in the materials through which their heroics can live on, whether these be poetry (ll.9-12) or history (l.16). But what engages him the most, and glows most deeply from within the poem, is his certainty that his lineage and his history will sustain him when he departs from Newstead for the larger world:

> "Shades of heroes, farewell! your descendant, departing
> From the seat of his ancestors, bids you, adieu!
> Abroad, or at home, your remembrance imparting
> New courage, he'll think upon glory, and you."

"Remembrance imparting new courage" is precisely what he sought and failed to find in "Childish Recollections." And unlike the later poem, here the past gives him a role he can play in the future:

> "That fame, and that memory, still will he cherish,
> He vows, that he ne'er will disgrace your renown;
> Like you will he live, or like you will he perish;
> When decay'd, may he mingle his dust with your own."

Some advice he gives to the Duke of Dorset in another poem echoes this attitude toward the past:

> "Turn to the annals of a former day,
> Bright are the deeds, thine earlier Sires display;
> One, tho' a Courtier, liv'd a man of worth,
> And call'd, proud boast! the British Drama forth.
> Another view! not less renown'd for Wit,
> Alike for courts, and camps, or senates fit;
> Bold in the field, and favour'd by the Nine,
> In ev'ry splendid part ordain'd to shine;
> Far, far distinguish'd from the glitt'ring throng,
> The pride of Princes, and the boast of Song.
> Such were thy Fathers, thus preserve their name,
> Not heir to titles only, but to Fame."
> "To the Duke of Dorset" (11.64-76)

Though Dorset's forbears are somewhat more illustrious (Thomas Sackville, the author of <u>Gorboduc</u>, for instance) than the odd mixture of actual and legendary ancestors that peoples "On Leaving Newstead Abbey," both poems are similarly disposed. Each attaches great value to poetry and to history. And, especially, each regards the past as a source of great power, at once to nourish the present and provide models to emulate in the future.

But the past that these poems consider is public and ancestral. In Byron's early poetry there are virtually no occasions on which a speaker approaches his personal past in anything like the manner I have just described. An isolated stanza or line sometimes points in that direction--perhaps "To Emma" is one such instance:

> "Well! we have pass'd some happy hours,
> And joy will mingle with our tears;

> When thinking on these ancient towers,
> The shelter of our infant years."
> (ll.9-12)

And these lines from "On a Distant View of the Village and School, of Harrow, on the Hill" would be another,

> "How welcome to me, your ne'er fading remembrance,
> Which rests in my bosom, though hope is deny'd."
> (ll.5-6)

if the poem did not begin,

> "Ye scenes of my childhood, whose lov'd recollection,
> Embitters the present, compar'd with the past."

These are, I think, the only *possible* examples. In poem after poem, remembrance is perceived just as it is in "Childish Recollections" and the "To Caroline" cycle, as an agent of pain and regret; and the past is a time that needs to be erased. The subject is addressed most directly in a short poem, appropriately titled "Remembrance":

> "'Tis done!--I saw it in my dreams:
> No more with Hope the future beams;
> My days of happiness are few:
> Chill'd by misfortune's wintry blast,
> My dawn of life is overcast,
> Love, Hope, and Joy, alike adieu!--
> Would I could add Remembrance too!"[13]

These lines are, perhaps, absurdly unspecific. But they circumscribe the attitude toward remembrance and the past that dominates all of the early poems that involve sustained recollection. For instance, immediately after the lines I quoted earlier from "To the Duke of Dorset," the speaker considers his own life:

> "The hour draws nigh, a few brief days will close,
> To me, this little scene of joys and woes;
> Each knell of Time now warns me to resign
> Shades, where Hope, Peace, and Friendship, all were mine;
> Hope, that could vary like the rainbow's hue,

> And gild their pinions, as the moments flew;
> Peace, that reflection never frown'd away,
> By dreams of ill, to cloud some future day;
> Friendship, whose truth let childhood only tell,
> Alas! they love not long, who love so well.
> To these adieu! nor let me linger o'er
>
> Scenes hail'd, as exiles hail their native shore,
> Receding, slowly, thro' the dark-blue deep,
> Beheld by eyes, that mourn, yet cannot weep."
> (ll.77-90)

It is probably not necessary to indicate how the final image presages Childe Harold as he sets out on his pilgrimage. Here, an "exile" from his past, he "mourns" and tries to forget ("nor let me linger o'er/Scenes hailed as exiles hail their native shore...").

A stanza from "Song" ("When I rov'd, a young Highlander, o'er the dark heath") effectively complements "On Leaving Newstead Abbey." It is personal and private about the same matters--his home, his lineage, his past and future--that the earlier poem treated publically and historically; it is diffident where the earlier poem was confident, peering backward as previously he looked forward:

> "I left my bleak home, and my visions are gone,
>   The mountains are vanish'd, my youth is no more;
> As the last of my race, I must wither alone,
>   And delight but in days, I have witness'd before;
> Ah! splendour has rais'd, but embitter'd my lot,
>   More dear were the scenes, which my infancy knew;
> Though my hopes may have fail'd, yet they are not
>   forgot,
>   Tho' cold is my heart, still it lingers with you."
> (ll.25-32)

In direct contrast to the public poems, which face the future with "great expectations," the poems that invoke the personal past invariably conclude with the speaker isolated and alone, at a loss for any real role to play.

"Epitaph on a Friend" was written in the same year as "On Leaving Newstead Abbey," and in *Hours of Idleness* was placed only one poem away from it.

> "Oh! Friend! for ever lov'd, for ever dear!
> What fruitless tears have bath'd thy honour'd bier!
> What sighs re-echo'd to thy parting breath,
> While thou wast struggling in the pangs of death!
> Could tears retard the tyrant in his course;
> Could sighs avert his dart's relentless force;
> Could youth and virtue claim a short delay,
> Or beauty charm the spectre from his prey;
> Thou still had'st lived, to bless my aching sight,
> Thy comrade's honour, and thy friend's delight;
> If, yet, thy gentle spirit hover nigh
> The spot, where now thy mould'ring ashes lie,
> Here, wilt thou read, recorded on my heart,
> A grief too deep to trust the sculptor's art.
> No marble marks thy couch of lowly sleep,
> But living statues, there, are seen to weep;
> Affliction's semblance bends not o'er thy tomb,
> Affliction's self deplores thy youthful doom.
> What though thy sire lament his failing line,
> A father's sorrows cannot equal mine!
> Though none, like thee, his dying hour will cheer,
> Yet other offspring soothe his anguish here:
> But, who with me shall hold thy former place?
> Thine image, what new friendship can efface?
> Ah! none! a father's tears will cease to flow,
> Time will assuage an infant brother's woe;
> To all, save one, is consolation known,
> While solitary Friendship sighs alone."

Despite its title, the poem, characteristically, is as engaged with the speaker's own perceptions and feelings. The first ten lines move back and forth between the qualities of his friend in death ("thy honour'd bier," "thy parting breath," "the pangs of death," etc.) and in life ("youth, "virtue," "beauty"), and the speaker's responses ("fruitless tears," "sighs," "tears," "sighs"), with an almost equal emphasis--almost, because the tragedy of the beautiful young man's death is finally perceived in terms of the speaker's own loss and deprivation: "Thou still had'st lived, to bless my aching sight,/Thy Comrade's honour, and thy friend's delight." The strained middle lines (ll.11-18) are another example of Byron's deep suspicion of the capacities of ordinary language, the same doubts he exercised so vigorously in the second "To Caroline" and in "To a Beautiful Quaker." Unable to commit his grief to straightforward and immediate phrases, he must resort to locutions like, "Here, wilt thou read, recorded on my heart,/A grief too deep to trust the sculptor's art," and the even more cumbersome, "Affliction's semblance bends not o'er thy tomb,/Affliction's self deplores thy youthful doom."

The poem turns upon two basic contrasts. The first is between the speaker and his dead friend's family, especially his father. Three times in the final section of the poem (ll.19-28), he asserts that his "sorrows," "anguish," and "woe" are greater than theirs. This is because, despite their closer blood ties, they have other roles to play--father, son, or brother. He had only one, friend, and the death of the young man has deprived him of this. The poem ends with him lost and alone, without a function or purpose:

> "To all, save one, is consolation known,
> While solitary Friendship sighs alone."

The other contrast is between the speaker and his friend. And here the drama is plotted in much the same way. The latter has a role--he is dead; the speaker, being friendless, again has none. The back and forth movements of the lines in the first section of the poem are perhaps enough to establish this. But a passage that appeared in <u>Poems</u> <u>on</u> <u>Various</u> <u>Occasions</u>, but was later cancelled, specifies the speaker's situation much more obviously:

> "Though low thy lot, since in a cottage born,
> No titles did thy humble name adorn;
> To me, far dearer, was thy artless love,
> Than all the joys, wealth, fame, and friends could
>   prove:
> For thee alone I liv'd, or wish'd to live,
> Oh God! if impious, this rash word forgive!
> Heart broken now, I wait an equal doom,
> Content to join thee, in thy turf-clad tomb;
> Where this frail form compos'd in endless rest,
> I'll make my last, cold, pillow on thy breast;
> That breast, where oft in life, I've laid my head,
> Will yet receive me mouldering with the dead;
> This life resign'd, without one parting sigh,
> Together in one bed of earth we'll lie!
> Together share the fate to mortals given,
> Together mix our dust and hope for Heaven."
> <u>POVO</u> (ll.11-28)

With greater emphasis, he points to the self-defining quality of this friendship, "For thee alone I liv'd, or wish'd to live." And as there is nothing else in his past that he can draw upon for sustenance ("This life resign'd, without one parting sigh"), he can think only of dying. In death he will again have a role that his life denies him:

> "Heart broken now, I wait an equal doom,
> Content to join thee, in thy turf-clad tomb...
> Together in one bed of earth we'll lie!
> Together share the fate to mortals given,
> Together mix our dust and hope for heaven."

"Stanzas" ("I would I were a careless child") is a virtual mirror image of this poem. It does not need to be examined in its entirety, but three stanzas, in particular, reenact the movement I have just described, with great exactitude.

>   3.
> "Few are my years, and, yet, I feel
>   The World was ne'er design'd for me,
> Ah! why do dark'ning shades conceal

>   The hour when man must cease to be?
>   Once I beheld a splendid dream,
>   A visionary scene of bliss;
>   Truth!--wherefore did thy hated beam
>   Awake me to a world like this?
>
>   4.
>   I lov'd--but those I lov'd, are gone,
>   Had friends--my early friends are fled,
>   How cheerless feels the heart alone,
>   When all its former hopes are dead!
>   Though gay companions, o'er the bowl,
>   Dispel awhile the sense of ill,
>   Though Pleasure stirs the maddening soul,
>   The heart--the heart is lonely still.
>
>   . . .
>
>   7.
>   Fain would I fly the haunts of men,
>   I seek to shun, not hate mankind,
>   My breast requires the sullen glen,
>   Whose gloom may suit a darken'd mind;
>   Oh! that to me the wings were given,
>   Which bear the Turtle to her nest!
>   Then would I cleave the vault of Heaven,
>   To flee away, and be at rest.

Once again the speaker is isolated and alone: "I lov'd--but those I lov'd, are gone...the heart is lonely still." His past was "a splendid dream,/A visionary scene of bliss"; but he is "awake," and the brilliance of the past, far from inspiring and fortifying his present life, embitters it, "Truth!--wherefore did thy hated beam/Awake me to a world like this?" As in the previous poem, he seems lost, as if he is on stage in a play which has no part for him--"I feel/The World was ne'er design'd for me"; and twice, in stanza three and in stanza seven, he expresses the desire to die.

In no single poem in these early collections is a speaker able to draw on his personal past to help him make his way "through a world like this." And, as in "Childish

Recollections," substitutes are developed, which permit him to escape from the "World that was ne'er designed for" him. Typically, there will be a shift in perspective to another kind of world, in which, by its very nature, all of the contradictions of his life are resolved and his difficulties simply vanish. Often, as in many of the poems I have been considering in this essay, a speaker will look forward to his death. One more poem of this character is "To M.S.G."

> "They tell us, that slumber, the sister of death,
>   Mortality's emblem is given;
> To fate how I long to resign my frail breath,
>   If this be a foretaste of Heaven."
>   (ll.9-12)

Another method of escaping the present, as in the second "To Caroline," is to take refuge in dreams. Again, from "To M.S.G.":

> "When I dream that you love me, you'd surely forgive
>   Extend not your anger to sleep;
> For, in visions alone, your affection can live,
>   I rise, and it leaves me to weep."
>   (ll.1-4)

Or in "Remind Me Not, Remind Me Not":

> "I dreamt last night our love return'd,
>   And sooth to say that very dream
>   Was sweeter in its phantasy
> Than if for other hearts I burn'd,
>   For eyes that ne'er like thine could beam
>   In rapture's wild reality."
>   (ll.25-30)[14]

"To a Beautiful Quaker" offers another example:

> "Thy form appears, through night, through day:
> Awake, with it my fancy teems,
> In sleep, it smiles in fleeting dreams;
> The vision charms the hours away,
> And bids me curse Aurora's ray;
> For breaking slumbers of delight,
> Which make me wish for endless night."
>   (ll.30-36)

Here he dreams away both night and day. The final line is
a witty play upon Catullus's <u>non est perpetua una dormienda</u> ("<u>Vivamus, mea Lesbia, atque amemus</u>"). What Catullus fears in the "endless night," Byron desires, because
he has delicately removed the metaphorical significance
of the image.

But preeminently the speakers of these early poems,
again as in "Childish Recollections," retreat into nostalgia, convinced that the past is the only place for them.
As "Stanzas" ("I would I were a careless child") bluntly
has it, "I ask but this--again to rove/Through scenes my
youth hath known before." A poem that is very much a companion piece to this one, in that both treat the Scottish
Highlands, and were composed at the same time, "Song"
("When I rov'd, a young Highlander, o'er the dark heath"),
expresses exactly the same sentiments:

>"More dear were the scenes which my infancy knew;
>Though my hopes may have fail'd, yet they are not
>   forgot.
>Tho' cold is my heart, still it lingers with you."
>   (ll.30-32)

"Pignus Amoris" begins this way:

>"As by the fix'd decrees of Heaven,
> 'Tis vain to hope that Joy will last;
>The dearest boon that Life has given,
> To me is--visions of the past."
>   (ll.1-4)

Nostalgia for the past is so efficacious a force in these
poems that occasionally it bursts forth in what can only
be called nostalgia for the future. That is, a speaker will
look forward to some possible future joy because, as he
experiences it, he will be reminded of the past. This can

be observed throughout the two long stanzas that conclude "Song" ("When I rov'd a young Highlander, o'er the dark heath"), beginning with, "When I see some dark hill point its crest to the sky,/I think of the rocks, that o'ershadow Colbeen." But it figures more strikingly in "On a Distant View of the Village and School, of Harrow, on the Hill":

>"But, if through the course of the years which
>   await me,
> Some new scene of pleasure should open to view,
> I will say, while with rapture the thought shall
>   elate me,
> 'Oh! such were the days, which my infancy knew.'"
>   (ll.33-36)

This is a precise inversion of the moment in "Childish Recollections" (ll.141-146) when the speaker tells us that he remembers how, as a boy, he anticipated remembering the events he is indeed recalling for us now.

One poem, "Lines Written Beneath an Elm, in the Churchyard of Harrow on the Hill," brings together all three ways of dispelling the present--death, dreams, and nostalgia--in a compact and forceful manner.

>"Spot of my youth! whose hoary branches sigh,
> Swept by the breeze that fans thy cloudless sky,
> Where now alone, I muse, who oft have trod,
> With those I lov'd, thy soft and verdent sod;
> With those, who scatter'd far, perchance, deplore,
> Like me the happy scenes they knew before;
> Oh! as I trace again thy winding hill,
> Mine eyes admire, my heart adores thee still,
> Thou drooping Elm! beneath whose boughs I lay,
> And frequent mus'd the twilight hours away;
> Where, as they once were wont, my limbs recline,
> But, ah! without the thoughts, which, then, were
>   mine;
> How do thy branches, moaning to the blast,
> Invite the bosom to recall the past,
> And seem to whisper, as they gently swell,
> 'Take, while thou canst, a ling'ring, last farewell!'
>
> When Fate shall chill at length this fever'd breast,

>   And calm its cares and passions into rest;
>   Oft, have I thought, 'twould soothe my dying hour,
>   If aught may soothe, when Life resigns her power;
>   To know, some humbler grave, some narrow cell,
>   Would hide my bosom, where it lov'd to dwell;
>   With this fond dream, methinks 'twere sweet to die,
>   And here it linger'd, here my heart might lie.
>   Here might I sleep, where all my hopes arose,
>   Scene of my youth, and couch of my repose;
>   Forever stretch'd beneath this mantling shade,
>   Prest by the turf, where once my childhood play'd;
>   Wrapt by the soil, that veils the spot I lov'd,
>   Mix'd with the earth, o'er which my footsteps mov'd;
>   Blest by the tongues, that charm'd my youthful ear,
>   Mourn'd by the few, my soul acknowledg'd here;
>   Deplor'd by those, in early days allied,
>   And unremember'd by the world beside.

This poem seems a kind of "condensed version" of the entire <u>Poems</u> <u>Original</u> and <u>Translated</u>, in which it first appeared. As so often, the speaker is "alone," thinking about his past, which is once again regarded as a source of regret: "With those, who scatter'd far, perchance, deplore,/Like me the happy scenes they knew before." He also emphasizes the differences between the past and present, and the distance he feels from his past: "Where, as they once were wont, my limbs recline,/But, ah! without the thoughts, which, then were mine." But these ambivalences do not prevent him from going on with his reminiscences or the poem. Finally, he turns to a consideration of his death.

    What is so remarkable about the "fond dream" he has of his death and burial is how elegantly it reconciles all of the contradications I have been describing, while at the same time underscoring just how fierce those contradictions are. The scene, once more, looks forward to <u>Wuthering</u> <u>Heights</u>. Just as the "love" between Heathcliff and Catherine could thrive only in childhood or in the grave, the speakers of Byron's early poems find the time between those two poles unbearable--"The present is hell!," "The world was ne'er design'd for me." But in the "fond dream" of his burial, he fuses past and future, leaping over what is in between, not <u>exactly dead</u> (in the final lines he seems very much alive; as Nelly Dean writes of Heathcliff, "I could not think him dead...I tried to close his eyes--to extinguish, if possible, that frightful, life-like gaze of exultation..."),[15] but at "rest"--at least for the moment, at least in this dream, at least for this poem.

> "Here might I sleep, where all my hopes arose,
> Scene of my youth, and couch of my repose;
> Forever stretch'd beneath this mantling shade,
> Prest by the turf, where once my childhood play'd;
> Wrapt by the soil, that veils the spot I lov'd,
> Mix'd with the earth, o'er which my footsteps mov'd;
> Blest by the tongues, that charm'd my youthful ear,
> Mourn'd by the few, my soul acknowledg'd here;
> Deplor'd by those, in early days allied,
> And unremember'd by the world beside."
>   (ll.25-34)

V

The ambivalences and contradictory attitudes that I have been describing in this essay also appear when the subject is poetry. Byron occasionally entertains the literary equivalent of wishing to die, giving up poetry. He is very explicit about this in the "Preface" which he wrote for <u>Hours of Idleness</u>. He tells his readers, "Poetry, however, is not my primary vocation; to divert the dull moments of indisposition, or the monotony of a vacant hour, urged me 'to this sin'; little can be expected from so unpromising a muse." He also announces that the volume will be his last: "With slight hopes and some fears, I publish this first and last attempt."[16]

But we really do not need the "Preface" to apprehend all this. The evidence is everywhere in the poems themselves. In almost all of the casual references to poetry and art, there is a recognition of a world of emotion and feeling that is beyond their reach. For instance, as we saw in "Epitaph on a Friend," he speaks of "A grief too deep to trust the sculptor's art." Or in "The Adieu" he writes: "How much thy friendship was above/Description's power of words!" Moreover, there is the deep suspicion of the material out of which poetry is fashioned that I have had occasion to glance at along the way. The second "To Caroline" and "To a Beautiful Quaker" conspicuously and directly identify language with deceit. Something like the same idea--the need for physical "symptoms" and "signs," not just words--organizes the opening lines of "The Tear":

> "When Friendship or Love
>   Our sympathies move;
> When Truth, in a glance, should appear,
>   The lips may beguile,
>   With a dimple or smile,
> But the test of affection's a Tear."
> (ll.1-6)

Consistent with this attitude toward language is his habit of insisting in many of his love poems that his inspiration is a real passion, not language or literary convention. Often he sounds rather like Astrophel venting his hostility against those poets who seem to be indulging a merely bookish fancy. Each of the first five stanzas of "The First Kiss of Love" shapes a contrast between two kinds of poetry, one--like romance or pastoral--which involves the working out of a literary tradition, and another, which he is practicing, that is based upon physical sensation.

> 1.
> "Away with your fictions of flimsy romance,
>   Those tissues of falsehood which Folly has wove;
> Give me the mild beam of the soul-breathing glance,
>   Or the rapture, which dwells on the first kiss of love.
>
> 2.
> Ye rhymers, whose bosomes with fantasy glow,
>   Whose pastoral passions are made for the grove;
> From what blest inspiration your sonnets would flow,
>   Could you ever have tasted the first kiss of love.
>
> 3.
> If Apollo should e'er his assistance refuse,
>   Or the Nine be dispos'd from your service to rove,
> Invoke them no more, bid adieu to the muse,
>   And try the effect, of the first kiss of love.
>
> 4.
> I hate you, ye cold compositions of art,
>   Tho' prudes may condemn me, and bigots reprove;
> I court the effusions, that spring from the heart,
>   Which throbs, with delight, to the first kiss of love.
>
> 5.
> Your shepherds, your flocks, those fantastical themes,
>   Perhaps, may amuse, yet they never can move;
> Arcadia displays but a region of dreams,
>   What are visions like these, to the first kiss of love?"
>
> (ll.10-20)

In "Stanzas to a Lady, with the Poems of Camoens," he makes precisely the same distinction. The reference is to Lord Viscount Strangford's Poems...of...Camoens: "He was in sooth, a genuine bard;/His was no faint fictitious flame." And in "To the Sighing Strephon" he sports with John Pigot for loving in too literary a manner. Previously Pigot had written some verses in which he complained that his lover was too coy. Byron responded with a poem of his own ("Reply to Some Verses of J.M.B. Pigot, Esq. on the Cruelty of his

Mistress"), that apparently offended Pigot. Here, he first apologizes for mistaking Pigot's conventional expressions of cruelty and despair for the real item:

>   3.
>   "Yet still, I must own,
>   I should never have known,
>   From your verses what else she deserv'd,
>   Your pain seem'd so great,
>   I pitied your fate,
>   As your fair was so dev'lish reserv'd."
>   (ll.13-18)

Then he facetiously appropriates some of Pigot's language, moving it to other contexts, and printing it in italics so as to be certain he won't miss the point:

>   4.
>   "Since the balm-breathing kiss,
>   Of this magical Miss,
>   Can such wonderful transports produce,
>   Since the 'world you forget,
>   When your lips once have met,'
>   My Counsel will get but abuse.
>
>   . . .
>
>   6.
>   I will not advance,
>   By the rules of romance,
>   To humour a whimsical fair,
>   Though a smile may delight,
>   Yet a frown won't affright,
>   Or drive me to dreadful despair.
>
>   . . .
>
>   8.
>   Though the kisses are sweet,
>   Which voluptuously meet,
>   Of kissing I ne'er was so fond,
>   As to make me forget,
>   Though our lips oft have met,
>   That still there was something beyond.
>
>   9.
>   And if I should shun,
>   Every woman for one,
>   Whose image must fill my whole breast;
>   Whom I must prefer,
>   And sigh but for her,

What an <u>insult</u> 'twould be to the <u>rest</u>."
(11.19-24; 31-36; 43-54)

Finally, he exposes the real source of Pigot's passion:

                10.
"No, Strephon, good bye,
 I cannot deny,
<u>Your passion</u> appears most absurd,
 Such <u>love</u> as you plead,
 Is <u>pure</u> love indeed,
For it <u>only</u> consists in the <u>word</u>."

Throughout all this, Byron has conveniently forgotten that his own claims to sincerity and immediacy are no less conventional, and have a tradition and a history.

    Again like Sidney, but for the most part, at this stage of his career, without the immense sophistication, Byron is anxious and uncertain about the vocabulary of love poetry. His love poems--and the "To Caroline" cycle is a good example of this--are rarely "about" the person he loves; the subject is invariably the speaker's attitudes, and the language that directs those attitudes. And there are a number of poems that explicitly address matters of literary style. "Lines Written in 'Letters of an Italian Nun and an English Gentleman'...Answer to the Foregoing, Address'd to Miss Pigot" appears to reverse the disposition toward language that we have now seen many times. It focuses upon a situation where language is conventional, flattering, and "true."

        Lines Written in 'Letters of an Italian Nun and
an English Gentleman', by J.J. Rousseau, Founded on Facts

    "'Away, away, your flattering arts
    May now betray some simpler hearts;
    And you will smile at their believing,
    And they shall weep at your deceiving.'"

Answer to the Foregoing, Address'd to Miss (Pigot)

"Dear simple girl, those flattering arts,
From which thou'dst guard frail female hearts,
Exist but in imagination,
Mere phantoms of thine own creation;
For he who views that witching grace,
That perfect form, that lovely face,
With eyes admiring, oh! believe me,
He never wishes to deceive thee:
Once in thy polish'd mirror glance,
Thou'lt there descry that elegance,
Which from our sex demands such praises,
But envy in the other raises.
Then he, who tells thee of thy beauty,
Believe me, only does his duty;
Ah! fly not from the candid youth,
It is not flattery, 'tis truth."

In "To the Sighing Strephon" or "To a Beautiful Quaker," it was a mark of great cleverness and sophistication to recognize and see through, as Miss Pigot does in her quatrain, "flattering arts," and the kind of language the speaker so blandly and expressionlessly records here that his smirk and snicker are all but imperceptible--"that witching grace," "that perfect form," "that lovely face." Ever more adroit and ingenious in his new role as the coy, sly, deadpan seducer ("Ah! fly not from the candid youth"), he turns her sophistication and good sense upside down, suggesting that her wariness demonstrates how "simple" she ultimately is--which, of course, she may be, should she fall for the "flattering art" that is this crafty little poem.

Another poem that plays with some of the conventions and traditions of literary love is "To a Lady, Who Presented to the Author a Lock of Hair, Braided with his Own, and Appointed a Night, in December, to Meet him in the

Garden." Like the second "To Caroline," it opens with
the speaker asserting the inferiority of merely verbal expressions of love to other kinds of evidence, as it were:

> "These locks, which fondly thus entwine,
> In firmer chains our hearts confine,
> Than all th' unmeaning protestations,
> Which swell with nonsense, love orations.
> Our love is fix'd, I think we've prov'd it,
> Nor time, nor place, nor art, have mov'd it;"
>
> (ll.1-6)

The locks of hair are somewhat more pragmatic than the "signs" of the earlier poem, with its "blushes," "sighs," and "murmurs," as demonstrably is the present speaker. In fact, the posture he advances is that of a man who is practical above all else, and, perhaps, nothing else. He is impatient and caustic before the "unmeaning protestations/ Which swell with nonsense, love orations"--including, one supposes, the many that appear alongside this poem and, less generally, a short piece addressed to the same unknown "Mary."[17] That piece is as unabashedly "romantic," as the speaker of "To a Lady" has it, as the latter is self-consciously sensible and matter of fact. There she also sends him a token designed to represent her love, a picture of herself, but entirely in keeping with Byron's practices and habits in these early poems, everything else about the dramatic situation, the point of view, and the attitudes toward love and poems of love is different:

> "Sweet copy! far more dear to me,
>   Lifeless, unfeeling as thou art,
> Than all the living forms could be,
>   Save her, who plac'd thee next my heart.
>
> She plac'd it, sad, with needless fear,

> Lest time might shake my wavering soul,
> Unconscious, that her image there,
> Held every sense in fast controul:
>
> Thro' hours, thro' years, thro' time, 'twill cheer;
> My hope, in gloomy moments, raise;
> In life's last conflict, 'twill appear,
> And meet my fond expiring gaze."
> (ll.17-28)

But his irritation with this style of writing--and the "To Caroline" cycle may offer even more precise examples--is not really that it is unfelt ("unmeaning") or that it is "nonsense," which is "unmeaning" in another sense. Preeminently, he objects to certain specific practical effects that it has had on one particular reader of it. It seems that "Mary," like many lovers in literature, as different as Don Quixote, Emma Bovary, young Romeo, the academics in Love's Labor's Lost, Alice Adams, and Woody Allen in Play It Again, Sam, has turned to other works of art for her information about love, and has learned--as Lorenz Hart writes in a song that also dallies with this tradition--"This can't be love/Because I feel so well./ No sobs, no sorrows, no sighs..."[18] Byron writes in a not dissimilar tone, spirit, and at times, even rhythm:

> "Then, wherefore, should we sigh, and whine,
> With groundless jealousy repine;
> With silly whims, and fancies frantic,
> Merely to make our love romantic?
> Why should you weep, like Lydia Languish,
> And fret with self-created anguish?"
> (ll.7-12)

But there is a more specific problem. When earlier he wrote, "Nor time, nor place, nor art have moved it," he was not as accurate as his confident, hard-headed inflections make him sound. For "art" has indeed "moved" their love, from the drawing room or bedroom right out into the cold:

> "Or doom the lover you have chosen,
> On winter nights, to sigh half frozen;
> In leafless shades, to sue for pardon,
> Only because the scene's a garden?
> For gardens seem, by one consent,
> Since SHAKESPEARE set the precedent,
> Since Juliet first declar'd her passion,
> To form the place of assignation."
> (11.12-20)

He weaves some of the texts he is complaining about into the fabric of the poem, moving from The Rivals to Romeo and Juliet, just as in the lines that immediately succeed these, he will allude to a "modern" corrective, Otway's Venice Preserved. Characteristically, in regard to Romeo and Juliet, he sports with a play that elsewhere he views with supreme seriousness. Some lines in the fourth "To Caroline" ("If again in the mansion of death I embrace thee,/Perhaps they will leave unmolested--the dead.") recall the final scenes of that play, as, of course, they also refer to Antony and Cleopatra.

For the rest of the poem, he urges "Mary" to set aside the ideas about love that she has received from books and plays, and love him in a manner more appropriate to the time and place. Along the way he makes sophisticated jokes about his own realism and pragmatism which, as the poem advances, become even more extreme and literal:

> "Oh! would some modern muse inspire,
> And seat her by a sea-coal fire;
> Or had the bard at Christmas written,
> And laid the scene of love in Britain;
> He surely, in commiseration,
> Had chang'd the place of declaration.
> In Italy, I've no objection;

> Warm nights are proper for reflection;
>
> . . .
>
> Or, if, at midnight, I must meet you,
> Within your mansion, let me greet you;
> There, we can love for hours together,
> Much better, in such snowy weather,
> Than plac'd in all th' Arcadian groves,
> That ever witness'd rural loves;
> There, if my passion fail to please,
> Next night I'll be content to freeze;
> No more I'll give a loose to laughter,
> But curse my fate, for ever after."
>
>   (ll.21-28; 35-44)

He playfully glances at the neo-classic concern with "imitation," which is promoted with much earnestness in "Hints from Horace" and "English Bards and Scotch Reviewers";

> "Think on our chilly situation,
>   And curb this rage for imitation;"
>   (ll.30-31)

And finally, though in an utterly different tone, he briefly rehearses the image we were left with at the end of the "To Caroline" cycle, of a world where love is all but impossible:

> "But, here, our climate is so rigid,
>   That love itself is rather frigid."
>   (ll.28-29)

Somewhat more seriously, a number of these early poems identify poetry with childhood in a fashion that could not readily have been predicted from the discussions of childhood, youth, and the past in "Childish Recollections," "To the Duke of Dorset," "On a Distant View of the Village and School, of Harrow, on the Hill," "Stanzas" ("I would I were a Careless Child"), "Song" ("When I rov'd a young Highlander, o'er the dark heath"), "The Tear," "To the Earl of Clare," and so many others. In each of these poems youth and childhood are directly, almost ostentatiously, equated with what Byron often simply and plainly calls "truth." Two related poems assert this even more unmistakably but with more sentimentality, I think, than any of the poems I have listed. In "To a Youthful Friend" he writes,

>"And when we bid adieu to youth
> Slaves to the specious world's control,
>We sigh a long farewell to truth;
> That world corrupts the noblest soul."
>   (ll.25-28)

And in "Pignus Amoris":

>"And Youth is sure the only time
> When Pleasure blends no base alloy;
>When life is blest without a crime,
> And innocence resides with Joy."
>   (ll.21-24)

But other poems subvert this identification with truth, representing it with some of the mirror's reversing powers--the same materials but not in the same relation to each other. Childhood and poetry ultimately emerge as just two more of the ideals which the restless voice that I have been describing "sees through." In "To Romance" all of the innocent qualities that the poems I catalogued above grant to youth and childhood are bitterly derided, and dismissed as illusions. It is necessary in the world of this poem to leave the "dreams," "deceit," and "affectation" of youth behind--in the name of "truth."

>   1.
>"Parent of golden dreams, Romance,
> Auspicious Queen! of childish joys,
>Who lead'st along in airy dance,
> Thy votive train of girls and boys;
>At length, in spells no longer bound,
> I break the fetters of my youth,

>   No more I tread thy mystic round,
>   But leave thy realms for those of Truth.
>   . . .
>   3.
>   And must we own thee, but a name,
>   And from thy hall of clouds descend?
>   Nor find a Sylph in every dame,
>   A Pylades in every friend;
>   But leave, at once, thy realms of air,
>   To mingling bands of fairy elves;
>   Confess that Woman's false as fair,
>   And friends have feeling for--themselves.
>   . . .
>   5.
>   Romance! disgusted with deceit,
>   Far from thy motley court I fly,
>   Where Affectation holds her seat,
>   And sickly Sensibility;
>   Whose silly tears can never flow,
>   For any pangs excepting thine,
>   Who turns aside from real woe,
>   To steep in dew thy gaudy shrine.
>   . . .
>   7.
>   Ye genial mymphs! whose ready tears,
>   On all occasions swiftly flow,
>   Whose bosoms heave with fancied fears,
>   With fancied flames and phrenzy glow;
>   Say, will you mourn my absent name,
>   Apostate from your gentle train?
>   An infant Bard at least may claim,
>   From you a sympathetic strain.
>   8.
>   Adieu, fond race, a long adieu,
>   The hour of fate is hov'ring nigh,
>   Even now the gulph appears in view,
>   Where unlamented you must lie;
>   Oblivion's blackening lake is seen,
>   Convuls'd by gales you cannot weather,
>   Where you, and eke your gentle queen,
>   Alas! must perish altogether."
>   (ll.1-8; 17-24; 33-40; 49-64)

In so many of the poems that I mentioned earlier, the wish was in some manner to return to the past. But here the speaker wants "to break the fetters of my youth./No more I tread thy mystic round,/But leave thy realms for those of

Truth." Of what the poems "of Truth" will be the speaker gives no indication. This poem is also retrospective and backward-looking. It re-"treads the mystic round," if only to keep claiming the author is getting off the treadmill. Probably the best commentary on this poem is a note Byron himself wrote as a gloss on line 20: "It is hardly necessary to add, that Pylades was the companion of Orestes, and a partner in one of those friendships, which with those of Achilles and Patroclus, Nisus and Euralus, Damon and Pythias, have been handed down to posterity, as remarkable instances of attachments, <u>which in all probability never existed</u> (my italics), beyond the imagination of the Poet, the page of an historian, or modern novelist."[19] It is also hardly necessary to add that Byron wrote poems in celebration of at least two of these famous male friendships.

One reason why even at the moment when it seems to be most called for (ll.53-56) he fails to describe his new poems "of Truth" is suggested by the "Preface" to <u>Hours of Idleness</u>. Often in this brief piece of prose he makes reference to his young age. He fears, for instance, that he "may incur the charge of presumption, for obtruding myself on the world, when without doubt, I might be, at my age, more usefully employed. These productions are the fruits of the lighter hours of a young man, who has lately completed his nineteenth year. As they bear the internal evidence of a boyish mind, this is, perhaps, unnecessary information." More tellingly, he writes in the final paragraph, a sentence of which I had occasion to quote earlier:

"With slight hopes, and some fears, I publish this first, and last attempt. To the dictates of young ambition, may be ascribed many actions more criminal, and equally absurd. To a few of my own age, the contents may afford amusement; I trust, they will, at least, be found harmless. It is highly improbable, from my situation, and pursuits hereafter, that I should ever obtrude myself a second time on the Public; nor even, in the very doubtful event of present indulgence, shall I be tempted to commit a future trespass of the same nature."[20]

Everywhere in the language of this "Preface"--"I might be, at my age, more usefully employed."; "Poetry, however, is not my primary vocation..."; "this first and last attempt..."; "the dictates of young ambition..."; "to a few of my own age..."; "from my situation and pursuits hereafter..."--are two related suggestions: that there will be no more poems, and this because writing poetry is what one does in childhood and youth. He more than intimates that once, in the manner of "To Romance," the illusions of youth have been dispelled, the world which poetry inhabits and describes also collapses. This is precisely the subject of a poem he wrote with the intention that it be his last, "Adieu to the Muse":[21]

1.
"Thou Power! who hast ruled me through infancy's days,
  Young offspring of Fancy, 'tis time we should part;
Then rise on the gale this the last of my lays,
  The coldest effusion which springs from my heart.

2.
This bosom, responsive to rapture no more,
  Shall hush thy wild notes, nor implore thee to sing;
The feelings of childhood, which taught thee to soar,
  Are wafted far distant on Apathy's wing.

3.
Though simple the themes of my rude flowing Lyre,
  Yet even those themes are departed for ever;

No more beam the eyes which my dream could inspire,
  My visions are flown, to return,--ah never!

4.

When drain'd is the nectar which gladdened the bowl,
  How vain is the effort delight to prolong!
When cold is the beauty which dwelt in my soul,
  What magic of Fancy can lengthen my song?

5.

Can the lips sing of Love in the desert alone,
  Of kisses and smiles which they now must resign?
Or dwell with delight on the hours that are flown?
  Ah, no! for those hours can no longer be mine.

6.

Can they speak of the friends whom I lived but to
    love?
  Ah, surely affection ennobles the strain!
But how can my numbers in sympathy move,
  When I scarcely can hope to behold them again?

7.

Can I sing of the deeds which my Fathers have done,
  And raise my loud harp to the fame of my Sires?
For glories like theirs, oh, how faint is my tone!
  For Heroes' exploits how unequal my fires!

8.

Untouch'd, then, my Lyre shall reply to the blast--
  'Tis hush'd; and my feeble endeavours are o'er;
And those who have heard it will pardon the past,
  When they know that its murmurs shall vibrate no
    more.

9.

And soon shall its wild erring notes be forgot,
  Since early affection and love is o'ercast:
Oh! blest had my fate been, and happy my lot,
  Had the first strain of love been the dearest, the
    last.

10.

Farewell, my young Muse! since we now can ne'er meet;
  If our songs have been languid, they surely are few:
Let us hope that the present at least will be sweet--
  The present--which seals our eternal Adieu."

As much as any single poem can, this shows us--paradoxically--Byron's "old" muse "seeing through" everything. Love, dreams, friendship, childhood and youth, memory, heroism, beauty, pleasure, and preeminently, poetry, have been experienced, examined, and been found wanting--discovered, most simply, not to be enough.

Of course this is not Byron's final poem. And perhaps the primary reason why he seems not to feel the need to characterize his poems "of truth," is that he has been writing them all along. The claims of "To Romance" to the contrary, Byron's early poetry is hardly the poetry of "dreams," "spells," "realms of air," and "fancied fears." Their total expression, however casual, playful, extreme, or extravagant any particular poem, is a surprisingly serious and powerful account of a restless, even relentless mind confronting its own conflicts and dilemmas. And perhaps at the base of these conflicts, which the poems do not pretend to resolve, are Byron's own doubts and uncertainties about himself as a poet, and the role and value of poetry. The drama of his early poetry is emphatically not simply "a young poet in search of his voice," though we encounter this along the way. According to the perspective, it is both larger and smaller than that. The motto of his family was "<u>Crede Byron</u>." But the quest in these poems is for something that Byron can believe--any "idea," "voice" or "role" that he can adopt unequivocally, without "seeing through" it.

VI

In this essay I have, for the most part, deliberately avoided the matter of whether these early poems should be called "autobiographical," and if the by turns ambivalent, contradictory, and radical attitudes they dramatize should be assigned to their author. Northrop Frye once wrote that "The main appeal of Byron's poetry is that it is Byron's... He proves what many critics claim to be impossible, that a poem can make its primary impact as a historical and biographical document."[22] I hope that in these pages I have demonstrated that this is not quite true, or that if it is, and the force of Byron's personality is unavoidably preeminent, we must not use this as a justification for not studying him in a spirit of, what he himself calls (though somewhat disparagingly), "<u>minute</u> or <u>verbal</u> criticism."[23] That I believe this is true for the early lyric poems as well as for <u>Childe Harold</u>, "Beppo" and <u>Don Juan</u> I also hope is evident, despite the fact that even the best recent books about Byron still read these poems only as "historical and biographical documents," or as uncertain territory to be rushed through on the way to some other place.

I have been considering Byron's practice of shifting perspective and point of view from poem to poem or within individual poems, as he examines, if finally to negate, larger and larger areas of experience. Certain other writers suggest themselves as analogies. I have already mentioned Sidney, whose <u>Astrophel and Stella</u> anticipates many features of these early poems. To summarize: a pervasive uncertainty about the vocabulary of poetry, especially the language of feeling; hostility toward those who seem to be writing about a merely literary love affair; perhaps most strikingly, a habit of attending to the changing attitudes of the speaker rather than to the attributes and qualities of the beloved; and, of course, the many poems that directly deal with aspects of style. Marvell is another. Perhaps the most common situation in his poetry is a debate between two or more developed and thoroughly articulated styles of living. For instance, "The Garden," "On a Drop of Dew," "Upon the Hill and Grove at Billborough," and "Upon Appleton House," from very different traditions and perspectives, argue the advantages of the active and meditative ways of life. Or "Young Love," "The Picture of Little T.C. in a Prospect of Flowers," "To His Coy Mistress" and "Ametas and Thestylis Making Hay-ropes" locate the carpe diem, carpe florem theme in an astonishing range of dramatic contexts. Marvell's "debates" also never conclude; their issues and conflicts are never resolved and settled. And after Byron there is Browning, whose dramatic monologues are triumphs of the kind of perspectivism I have been describing here. Also, he published many of his poems in pairs ("My Last Duchess" and "Count Gismond"; "The Laboratory" and "The Confessional"; "The Italian in England" and "The Englishman in Italy," and numerous others), attending to contrary aspects of the same subject or style. Finally, Byron's poem "The Giaour," with its differing and contradictory accounts of the same events, very much anticipates The Ring and the Book.

But the central difference between these poets and Byron in his early poetry (not, I would argue, in Don Juan, and the studied, even stagey letters) is the poise and ease with which they encounter and dramatize conflicts, contradictions, and irreconcilable perspectives and points of view, and Byron's desperation about these matters. His version of the "debate" situation perhaps finds its best expression in the opening stanza of his translation of some lines from The Medea of Euripides:

> "When fierce conflicting passions urge
>   The breast, where love is wont to glow,
> What mind can stem the stormy surge,
>   Which rolls the tide of human woe?
> The hope of praise, the dread of shame,
>   Can rouse the tortur'd breast no more;
> The wild desire, the guilty flame,
>   Absorbs each wish it felt before."
>   (ll.1-8)

"When fierce conflicting passions urge" could serve as a motto for these early poems. And the self-consuming passions of the final lines reenact the drama of the Titan's breakfast, but in a darker tone. Characteristically (both of Byron and the poets I have compared him to), he goes on to undercut his impetuous attitude in the succeeding stanza:

> "But, if affection gently thrills
>   The soul, by purer dreams passest,
> The pleasing balm of mortal ills,
>   In love can soothe the aching heart,
> If thus, thou com'st in gentle guise
>   Fair Venus! from thy native heaven,
> What heart, unfeeling, would despise
>   The sweetest boon the gods have given?"
>   (ll.9-16)

And, again indicatively, he contradicts this in the lines that immediately follow ("The wild desire...absorbs each wish it felt before."), and we are right back where we started:

> "But, never from thy golden bow,
>   May I beneath the shaft expire,
> Whose creeping venom, sure and slow

>   Awakes an all-consuming fire..."
>   (ll.17-20)

This poem was also written in the same year as "To Romance," and placed a few pages away from it in Hours of Idleness; there, as we saw, he dismisses the issue entirely. Finally, characteristic of himself alone, in another poem written the same year, and which quotes from his translation of The Medea, he returns to his "fierce conflicting passions" in accents that directly prefigure Childe Harold:

> Damaetas
>
>   "In law an infant, and in years a boy,
>   In mind a slave to every vicious joy,
>   From every sense of shame and virtue wean'd,
>   In lies an adept, in deceit a friend;
>   Vers'd in hypocrisy, while yet a child,
>   Fickle as wind, of inclinations wild;
>   Woman his dupe, his heedless friend a tool,
>   Old in the world, though scarcely broke from school;
>   Damaetas ran through all the maze of sin,
>   And found the goal, when others just begin:
>   Ev'n still conflicting passions shake his soul,
>   And bid him drain the dregs of pleasure's bowl;
>   But, pall'd with vice, he breaks his former chain,
>   And, what was once his bliss, appears his bane."

II

Disporting There Like Any Other Fly

Most readers of Cantos I and II of Childe Harold's Pilgrimage, from Dallas and Murray down to the present day, have identified inconsistencies in attitude and tone.[1] Their observations are exactly right. The Cantos offer distinctly contradictory reflections on war, love, poetry, time, the purpose and value of a pilgrimage, and virtually all of the other subjects they consider. But not so widely noticed is the manner in which the poem consistently and carefully serves to undermine the very idea of consistency, and any effort--including those it has occasion to indulge along the way--to engage the world systematically. Childe Harold is an arrangement of voices, an instance of what Mahler once called a "ruthless contrapuntal technique." The arrangement is fundamentally dramatic. That is, the various voices of the poem interact with one another, comment upon each other, take up the same topics from different perspectives and points of view, expose their respective limitations, parody one another, and occasionally drown each other out. The drama of Childe Harold's Pilgrimage is so precisely calculated that conceivably it could be staged; it is a wonder that more have not been tempted to refashion that drama in music.

Although there are as many as six speakers in the first two Cantos, only three figure to any significant degree.[2] At the center, with the fewest lines but with a presence and a prominence that belies his relative silence, is Childe Harold. A narrator follows Harold through his travels; he is as energetic and opinionated as his subject is detached and indifferent. Lastly, at cross purposes to the narrator, is a third voice that seeks to place the former's circumstantial and occasional concerns in a larger and comic perspective--comic in the sense of the conclusion of Chaucer's Troilus and Cressida, or Shakespeare's fools, or Don Juan--but ultimately is unable to. As he writes "unavailing woe/Bursts from my heart, and mingles with the strain" (I.91). A large part of the power and accomplishment of Byron's performance in Childe Harold resides in the way he "plays off" these voices, one against the others, and in the timing of his transitions, as he moves from voice to voice.

The diction and posture of the narrator is drawn in equal measure from some of the long poems that Byron admired as a young man, Thomson's Castle of Indolence, Beattie's The Minstrel and White's The Christriad and the novels of Smollett and Fielding. Many of the attributes that characterize him throughout the poem are present in the second stanza, which is also where he speaks for the first time.

> Whilome in Albion's isle there dwelt a youth,
> Who ne in virtue's ways did take delight;
> But spent his days in riot most uncouth,
> And vex'd with mirth the drowsy ear of Night.
> Ah me! in sooth he was a shameless wight,
> Sore given to revel and ungodly glee;
> Few earthly things found favour in his sight
> Save concubines and carnal companie,
> And flaunting wassailers of high and low degree.
> (I.2)

His range must not be circumscribed too narrowly. As he proceeds from phrase to phrase, he is alternately a jaunty, worldly appreciator of folly, capable of humorous and self-mocking interjections ("Ah, me!"), and a stern moralist who does not flinch before absolute judgements ("shameless wight," "unworldly glee"). Similarly, the antique phrasing is at once a way of tapping into a moral tradition that leads back to Spenser and Chaucer (as in Thomson and White), and a source of deft comic touches. This flexibility of tone and vocabulary distinguishes the early stanzas of the poem especially. In the passage that describes Harold's home, for instance, he includes a fine joke about its age:

> "It was a vast and venerable pile;
> So old, it seemed only not to fall..."

And he sports with the reputation for lasciviousness of the monks who once dwelled there:

> "Now Paphian girls were known to sing and smile;
> And monks might deem their time was come agen,
> If ancient tales say true, nor wrong these holy men."

But he places his enthusiastic disapproval precisely in the center of the stanza: "Monastic dome! Condemn'd to uses vile!" (I.7)

In these two poised stanzas the narrator effects a kind of balance between his impulse to follow a good story--Harold's dissolution, the monks' wantonness--for its own sake, and his eagerness to pass judgment. But elsewhere in the poem it is usually one attitude or the other which dominates at any particular point. "Whilome" is among the many self-defining idioms and formulas he employs to propel his stories forward. Others include "It chanc'd that..." (II.67), "It came to pass..." (II.69), "Childe Harold was he hight..." (I.3), and "Ye who shall marvel when you hear her tale..." (I.55). And the animated storyteller is prominent in the

Bullfight stanzas (I.72-80), for example, or in those concerned with Albania (II.46-72). Much more commonly and regularly, however, it is the moralist who has the upper hand in the narrative: and it is through the filter of his exacting moral sense that the incidents of Harold's travels principally are revealed to us.

One consequence of this moral bias is that, despite his accustomed suppleness of tone and diction, the narrator invariably condemns Childe Harold. An occasional passage will hint at a quiet sympathy:

>"Yet deem not thence his breast a breast of steel:
>Ye, who have known what 'tis to doat upon
>A few dear objects, will in sadness feel
>Such partings break the heart they fondly hope to heal."
>(I.10)

And with a seemingly more intense and particular focus:

>"(Harold) had sigh'd to many though he lov'd but one,
>And that lov'd one, alas! could ne'er be his."

But as the effect of the first is more than a little diffused by the uncertain fix that it has on Harold (note how he disappears from the lines, and they do not so much describe him as appeal to the experience of certain readers: "Ye, who have known..."), so the empathy of the other is overwhelmed by the sharp, pointed disapproval that directs the stanza in which it appears:

>"For he through Sin's long labyrinth had run,
>Nor made atonement when he did amiss,
>Had sigh'd to many though he lov'd but one,
>And that lov'd one, alas!could ne'er be his.
>Ah, happy she! to 'scape from him whose kiss
>Had been pollution unto aught so chaste;
>Who soon had left her charms for vulgar bliss,
>And spoil'd her goodly lands to gild his waste,
>Nor calm domestic peace had ever deign'd to taste."
>(I.5)

His language here recalls many of Byron's early poems, but especially "Damaetas" and "Childish Recollections." The phrases that mark religious censure ("Sin's long labyrinth," "Nor made atonement when he did amiss," "pollution"), and the words that seem to draw upon Shakespeare's vocabulary in the <u>Sonnets</u> ("spoil'd," "to gild," "waste") figure consistently in the narrator's apprehension of Harold throughout the poem. At the start he is, as we have seen, "a shameless wight"; he has been "drugg'd...with pleasure" (I.6); and "His early youth (was) mispent in maddest whim." (I.27) As late as the second Canto, he is described as "not unskilful in the spoiler's art,/And spread its snares licentious far and wide..." (II.35). Along the way, he is identified with Cain and, through him, with Coleridge's Ancient Mariner:[3]

>"And Vice, that digs her own voluptuous tomb,
>Had buried long his hopes, no more to rise:
>Pleasure's pall'd victim! life-abhorring gloom
>Wrote on his faded brow curst Cain's unresting doom."
>   (I.83)

The narrator's moral and religious convictions also incline him to direct the particulars of Harold's travels into a coherent whole, possessing a clear beginning, conclusion, and purpose, as well as a consistent development and shape. As I hope to argue more extensively below, Harold sees little in his journey beyond aimless wandering. He seeks only diversion, a "change of scene" (I.6). In his "Good night" he dispenses with the notion of a goal:

>"With thee, my bark, I'll swiftly go
>   Athwart the foaming brine;
>Nor care what land thou bear'st me to,
>   So not again to mine.

> Welcome, welcome, ye dark-blue waves!
> And when you fail my sight,
> Welcome, ye deserts, and ye caves!
> My native Land--Good Night!"
> (13)

But his narrator has other ideas. Three times in the course of the first Canto he refashions Harold's careless excursions ("Nor care I what land thou bear'st me to...") into what he terms a "pilgrimage" (10, 28, 93); and "pilgrim" is one of his prevailing appellations for his hero (I.43, II.50 and 64). In his own eyes, Harold is a "pilgrim" because he is a person on a journey or because he travels from place to place. For the narrator, "pilgrimage" is invested with connotations that are fundamentally religious in nature and design. Perhaps only the determined patriotism he manifests in the stanzas on Cintra (I.24-26) and on Elgin (II.11-14) is more conventional than his dispositions on this matter. A "pilgrimage" has its origins in heartsickness--"And now Childe Harold was sore sick at heart" (I.6)--and in the acknowledgement of sin (I.5), and the grim blankness of worldly pleasures:

> "But long ere scarce a third of his pass'd by,
> Worse than adversity the Childe befell;
> He felt the fulness of satiety:
> Then loath'd he in his native land to dwell,
> Which seem'd to him more lone than Eremite's sad cell."
> (I.4)

The "pilgrim" has unambiguous if general goals. In a section I quoted earlier, Harold is represented as departing from his home in order that he might be healed (I.10). Elsewhere he is in search of "peace" or, more often, "rest." Both words appear in a stanza which offers a contrast between the narrator's interpretation of the "pilgrimage" and Childe Harold's.

> "To horse! to horse! he quits, for ever quits
> A scene of peace, though soothing to his soul:
> Again he rouses from his moping fits,
> But seeks not now the harlot and the bowl.
> Onward he flies, nor fix'd as yet the goal
> Where he shall rest him on his pilgrimage;
> And o'er him many changing scenes must roll
> Ere toil his thirst for travel can assuage,
> Or he shall calm his breast, or learn experience sage."
> (I.28)

Typically, Harold only desires to move on. The narrator actively regrets his departure, preferring that he linger in a "scene of place"; that way, his soul may be "soothed." The Childe has not "fix'd as yet the goal/Where he shall rest him on his pilgrimage," but the narrator cannot imagine that his restlessness or wandering could endure indefinitely, even though he places the conclusion in the distant future ("And o'er him many changing scenes must roll..."). The final lines expand upon the previous senses of "pilgrimage," suggesting that in addition to "rest" ("toil...can assuage," and "he shall calm his breast") there will be an intensification of knowledge at the journey's end as well. Each of these guiding conceptions appears in even the most casual of the narrator's descriptions of Harold's peregrinations. Places of "rest" and "peace" are identified and pursued, and occur with greater frequency as the poem continues:

> "Then slowly climb the many-winding way,
> And frequent turn to linger as you go,
> From loftier rocks new loveliness survey,
> And rest ye at our 'Lady's house of woe';"
> (I.20)

> "Here in the sultriest season let him rest,
> Fresh is the green beneath those aged trees;
> Here winds of gentlest wing will fan his breast,
> From heaven itself he may inhale the breeze:

> The plain is far beneath--oh! let him seize
> Pure pleasure while he can; the scorching ray
> Here pierceth not, impregnate with disease:
> Then let his length the loitering pilgrim lay,
> And gaze, untir'd, the morn, the noon, the eve away."
> (II.50)

> "'Mid many things most new to ear and eye
> The pilgrim rested here his weary feet..."
> (II.64)

> "Vain fear! the Suliotes stretch'd the welcome hand...
> Such conduct bears Philanthropy's rare stamp--
> To rest the weary and to soothe the sad,
> Doth lesson happier men, and shames at least the bad."
> (II.68)

And Harold, again increasingly as the poem goes on, is perceived as one of those "happier men," not so much "shamed" now as "lessoned." The narrator often reports on his progress:

> "Though here awhile he learn'd to moralize,
> For Meditation fix'd at times on him;
> And conscious Reason whisper'd to despise
> His early youth, mispent in maddest whim;"
> (I.27)

> "And lately had he learn'd with truth to deem
> Love has no gift so grateful as his wings:
> How fair, how young, how soft soe'er he seem
> Full from the font of Joy's delicious springs
> Some bitter o'er the flowers its bubbling venom flings"
> (I.82)

Ultimately, from the perspective of the narrator, the countries through which Harold passes, and the scenes that he is witness to, assume the weight and expressiveness that shrines and holy places have for other kinds of pilgrims. They do not divert merely, or even captivate; they have the power to instruct and to change those who encounter them:

> "Yet to the remnants of thy splendour past
> Shall pilgrims, pensive, but unwearied, throng...

> Boast of the aged! lesson of the young!
>
> . . .
>
> He that is lonely hither let him roam,
> And gaze complacent on congenial earth."
> (II.91-92)

These efforts of the narrator to fashion a familiar pattern from Harold's life and travels are undermined, belied, and rendered suspect by other aspects of his rhetorical habits. First of all, despite his confident assessment of the Childe's character and the blithe account of his growth and advances, the narrator seems to know remarkably little about him. A sense of uncertainty, of dim, immutable obscurity informs almost all of his descriptions of Harold. Early in the poem he strikes a posture of coy speculation:

> "Childe Harold was he hight:--but whence his name
> And lineage long, it suits me not to say;
> Suffice it, that perchance they were of fame,
> And had been glorious in another day:
> But one sad losel soils a name for aye,
> However mighty in the olden time;
> Nor all that heralds rake from coffin'd clay,
> Nor florid prose, nor honied lies of rhyme,
> Can blazon evil deeds, or consecrate a crime."
> (I.3)

He begins the stanza appearing to withhold information for certain unstated, private reasons: "it suits me not to say"; then he combines this attitude ("suffice it, that...") with what he openly identifies as conjecture ("perchance"); lastly, as in stanza 10, he retreats into abstract moralizing that has nothing to do with Harold and his family (11.5-9), if only because he has refused to discuss them plainly and directly. The narrator's assured tone in these final lines, with their suggestive adjectives and striking verbs, the grand flights of time and space ("for aye," "in the olden time," "all that heralds rake"), and the rush of seemingly indisputable statements almost allows us to overlook the absence of Harold and his ancestors.

Other stanzas perform a variation upon this pattern of assertion and withdrawal:

> "Yet oft-times in his maddest mirthful mood
> Strange pangs would flash along Childe Harold's brow,
> As if the memory of some deadly feud
> Or disappointed passion lurk'd below:
> But this none knew, nor haply car'd to know;
> For his was not that open, artless soul
> That feels relief by bidding sorrow flow,
> Nor sought he friend to counsel of condole,
> Whate'er his grief mote be, which he could not control."
> (I.8)

Here a hazy and skeletal reference--"strange pangs"-- is, by means of an almost silent "As if," very nimbly fleshed out, and not only is given a body, but a history as well: "the memory of some deadly feud/Or disappointed passion lurk'd below." In the next line the narrator appears to be recoiling from what he has just said and to be acknowledging its status as speculation ("But this none knew"). But our attention is carefully directed away from his limitations and back to Harold. When he says, "nor haply car'd to know," the suggestion is that he, like everyone else, does not know because he does not wish to; and moreover, who would care to traffic in the kinds of memories and emotions that can be depicted as "lurk(ing) below"? Similarly, the lines that follow do not really offer a second explanation for his lack of knowledge. For even as he is asserting that "(Harold's) was not that open, artless soul," he is craftily and tendentiously opening up that soul, as it were, and identifying what he finds there--"sorrow," or "grief," which might benefit from "counsel" or "condolence," as it is manifestly beyond his "control." On other occasions the narrator forthrightly adopts the formulas of the gossip,"'Tis said," "seemed," and "it may be":

> "'Tis said, at times the sullen tear would start,
> But Pride congeal'd the drop within his ee"
> (I.6)

> And then, it may be, of his wish to roam
> Repented be, but in his bosom slept
> The silent thought..."
> (I.12)

Each of these devices permits the narrator to make strong declarations about Harold's thoughts and actions even as he asserts (though less loudly and vigorously) that he has no grounds for voicing them. By these means he obscures his distance from the Childe, disguises his want of sure information, and puts a mask upon his unreliability.

If these strategies tend to beguile the reader, certain of the narrator's other practices serve to lead *him* astray and, unwittingly, to trip him up. Often he does not appear to be entirely certain of what he wishes to be saying, and expresses more than he evidently intends to. In contrast to Harold, he is usually excited and animated by what the journey sets before him; but his enthusiasm can induce him to become rather involved in matters that he disapproves of, and the consequences are humorous. This is what happens in the bullfight stanzas (I.62-80). He begins with a discussion of the fashionable pursuits that occupy the citizens of Cadiz and London on Sundays.

> "The Sabbath comes, a day of blessed rest;
> What hallows it upon this Christian shore?
> Lo! it is sacred to a solemn feast:
> Hark! heard you not the forest-monarch's roar?
> Crashing the lance, he snuffs the spouting gore
> Of man and steed, o'erthrown beneath his horn;
> The throng'd Arena shakes with shouts for more;
> Yells the mad crowd o'er entrails freshly torn,
> Nor shrinks the female eye, nor ev'n affects to mourn.
>
> The seventh day this; the jubilee of man.
> London! right well thou know'st the day of prayer:
> Then thy spruce citizen, wash'd artizan,
> And smug apprentice gulp their weekly air:
> Thy coach of Hackney, whiskey, one-horse chair,
> And humblest gig through sundry suburbs whirl,
> To Hampstead, Brentford, Harrow make repair;
> Till the tir'd jade the wheel forgets to hurl,
> Provoking envious gibe from each pedestrian Churl.
>
> Some o'er thy Thamis row the ribbon'd fair,
> Others along the safer Turnpike fly;
> Some Richmond-hill ascend, some scud to Ware,
> And many to the steep of Highgate hie.
> Ask ye, Boeotian shades! the reason why?
> 'Tis to the worship of the solemn Horn,
> Grasp'd in the holy hand of Mystery,
> In whose dread name both men and maids are
>   sworn,
> And consecrate the oath with draught, and dance till
>   morn.
>
> All have their fooleries--not alike are thine,
> Fair Cadiz, rising o'er the dark blue sea!
> Soon as the matin bell proclaimeth nine,
> Thy saint adorers count the rosary:
> Much is the VIRGIN teaz'd to shrive them free
> (Well do I ween the only virgin there)
> From crimes as numerous as her beadsmen be;
> Then to the crowded circus forth they fare,
> Young, old, high, low, at once the same diversion share.
>
> The lists are op'd, the spacious area clear'd,
> Thousands on thousands pil'd are seated round;
> Long ere the first loud trumpet's note is heard,
> Ne vacant space for lated wight is found:
> Here dons, grandees, but chiefly dames abound,
> Skill'd in the ogle of a roguish eye,
> Yet ever well inclin'd to heal the wound;
> None through their cold disdain are doom'd to die,
> As moon-struck bards complain, by Love's sad archery."
>   (I.68-72)

Thomas Moore, perhaps taking his cue from a letter that Byron wrote to Dallas in which he discusses this passage, believed that the presence of the two stanzas on London "disfigure(d) the poem."[4] Indeed this is one of the few occasions on which the narrator is deliberately funny. But the joke extends much farther than he realizes, and the role that is defined for him here is entirely consistent with the way he is perceived throughout <u>Childe Harold</u>. Though he condemns both London and Cadiz, the censure of the former is only ironic. While this is a world in which "All have their fooleries," there are differences of degree and kind, and "not alike are thine,/ Fair Cadiz." The narrator intends, then, to contrast the two cities, not to seek resemblances. In fact, it is the supposed affinities that secure his opposition between the violent entertainment of the Spaniards and gentler practices of the Londoners. As he moves back and forth from one city to the other--their respective "horns," their crowds and the sounds they make, their choice of animals, the physical excesses, and numerous minute echoes (the repetition of "solemn," the pun that derives "morn" from "mourn," the "horn" rhymes in 68 and 70, the "prayer" rhymes in 69 and 71, the "fly" rhymes in 70 and 72, etc.)--the fine web of connections and parallels demonstrates the disparities he wishes us to see, and seems to justify his conclusion that they are "not alike."

But there is a kind of counter-movement to this in the lines that the narrator neither controls nor perceives.

His carefully modulated and fastidious efforts to derive dissimilarity from apparent identity has led him to overlook certain larger connections between the two cities which fall outside of his precise scheme. And as the passage continues (71-72), the correspondences become overwhelming. The "worship of the solemn Horn,/Grasp'd in the holy hand of Mystery" no longer seems so innocent when placed beside the prayers to the Virgin before the bullfight or the actions of the "dames" in the arena: taken together these are its exact counterpart. London and Cadiz combine religious hypocrisy with a cynical attitude toward love; in each cuckoldry is the established form of worship.

After the bullfight starts the narrator is on no more solid ground. Though he has already indicated his disapproval, he is quickly drawn into the action. A few brief references to the attending crowds bespeak an effort to distance himself from the scene (73), and he pauses to sympathize with the matador's horse (74); but otherwise his response is uncomplicatedly ardent and approving. This extends to every element of the spectacle: the strength, ferocity, and intelligence of the bull--

> "And, wildly staring, spurns, with sounding foot,
> The sand, nor blindly rushes on his foe:
> Here, there, he points his threatening front, to suit
> His first attack, wide waving to and fro
> His angry tail; red rolls his eye's dilated glow."
> (75)

He calls out to the matador:

> "Away, thou heedless boy! prepare the spear:
> Now is thy time, to perish, or display
> The skill that yet may check his mad career."
> (76)

The horse in his death throes is now more admired than pitied:

> "Another, hideous sight! unseam'd appears,
> His gory chest unveils life's panting source,
> Tho' death-struck still his feeble frame he rears,
> Staggering, but stemming all, his lord unharm'd he bears."
> (77)

And he describes the killing of the bull in this manner:

> "Foil'd, bleeding, breathless, furious to the last,
> Full in the centre stands the bull at bay,
> Mid wounds, and clinging darts, and lances brast,
> And foes disabled in the brutal fray:
> And now the Matadores around him play,
> Shake the red cloak, and poise the ready brand:
> Once more through all he burst his thundering way--
> Vain rage! the mantle quits the conynge hand,
> Wraps his fierce eye--'tis past--he sinks upon the sand!
> (78)

For more than seven stanzas the narrator loses himself in the actions he is dramatizing. Each aspect of his performance, from the punctuation and pacing to the individual word choices, points to his absorption and enthusiasm. It is not until the corpse of the bull is put on display, and he is forced to notice the reaction of the other spectators, that he remembers what he really thinks about bullfighting: "The decorated car appears--on high/The corse is pil'd--sweet sight for vulgar eyes..." (79). The dashes seem to mark the stages in his reawakening. The lines allude to The Aeneid, VIII.264-265; he withdraws by shaping a facetious comparison between the matador and Hercules. Then, fully recovered, he goes on, as if nothing has happened, to say the proper things about the Spaniards and their love of violent amusement:

> "Such the ungentle sport that oft invites
> The Spanish maid, and cheers the Spanish swain.
> Nurtur'd in blood betimes, his heart delights
> In vengeance, gloating on another's pain."
> (80)

The narrator's inability to comprehend fully the implications of his statements and enthusiasms leads, as we have seen here, into many stanzas of unintentional self-parody. One other feature of his style makes him particularly prone to this effect--his reliance on what is probably best termed pastiche. Often his lines and sentences have been worked up from a number of brief, and not especially forward allusions. One stanza that I cited earlier (I.2), for instance, makes use of Shakespeare's King John, Thomson's Castle of Indolence, Burns' "Author's Earnest Cry and Prayer," and Beattie's The Minstrel--all in two lines (ll.4-5).[5] These allusions, as far as the narrator is concerned, are discrete and self-contained. They do not require that we return to the original texts for aid in understanding a passage, and they do not expand his narrative significantly. He appeals not to a context but a phrase. "And vex'd with mirth the drowsy ear of Night" reminds us of, "Sound on into the drowsy race of night" and "Life is as tedious as a twice-told tale/Vexing the dull ear of a drowsy man...." but glances at nothing else in Shakespeare's play. These allusions appear to be the product of an aspect of his personality that is most strikingly captured in Don Juan: "and what's travel/Unless it teaches one to quote and cavil?"

But on occasion, this refusal to attend to the context

of an allusion or a quotation results in the betrayal of the effect he is attempting to achieve, in a manner that is reminiscent of the frustrated contrast between London and Cadiz. For example, in the midst of his hearty glowing tribute to the martial spirit and skills of the women of Spain is this stanza:

> "Is it for this the Spanish maid, arous'd,
> Hangs on the willow her unstrung guitar,
> And, all unsex'd, the Anlace hath espous'd,
> Sung the loud song, and dar'd the deed of war?
> And she, whom once the semblance of a scar
> Appall'd, an owlet's 'larum chill'd with dread,
> Now views the column-scattering bay'net jar,
> The falchion flash, and o'er the yet warm dead
> Stalks with Minerva's step where Mars might quake
>   to tread."
>   (54)

He manifestly wishes to continue his praise here. When he says that the Spanish maid is "all unsexed," he means that she has adopted the attitudes and actions usually associated with more war-like males; and to show how far she has come, he tells us that "once...an owlet's 'larum chill'd (her) with dread." In order to promote his sense of her heroic status he draws upon two speeches in <u>Macbeth</u>: "unsex me here..." (I.V), and "The time has been, my senses would have cool'd/To hear a night-shriek..." (V.V). But the circumstances of the allusions, beyond the power of the individual words, cast the Spanish maid in a much harsher light than he recognizes. In one a woman seeks inspiration before committing a murder of "direst cruelty"; in the other a murderer notes how his deeds have jaded him-- "I have supped full of horrors." They undermine the force of his admiration, and introduce unintended touches of strangeness and perversity. Similarly, the bold image which concludes the stanza is undone by the line that trots behind it, Pope's "For Fools rush in where Angels fear to tread."

The speaker of the passages I have been discussing belongs to a tradition of limited and untrustworthy narrators that stretches back at least to The Satyricon and, of course, is conspicuous in much of the eighteenth-century fiction that Byron prized. One of the abiding impulses in Childe Harold is this thwarting of the narrator's designs, which at once deflates his earnest, restricted vision and introduces a different point of view. In these stanzas, for instance, we have been apprised of the depravation that resides in London and Cadiz, and the debasements that have been brought about by the Spanish wars, although the narrator has been tugging us in other directions. But above this impulse, these time-bombs that have been planted in his rhetoric, there is a second voice in the poem which expands upon it. This voice is comic in two senses: its relationship with the narrator is customarily a humorous one, and it seeks to place the latter's narrow concerns within a larger perspective. For what is true of the allusions is also the case in the poem as a whole. The narrator's focus is always local--the situations he encounters and the subjects he discusses are always only ends in themselves; but the comic voice steps back, insists upon a wider vista, and regards them as examples.

In the second Canto, the narrator is enraged by the actions of Lord Elgin, and energetically condemns his "plunder":

> "But who, of all the plunderers of yon fane
> On high, where Pallas linger'd, loth to flee
> The latest relic of her ancient reign;
> The last, the worst, dull spoiler, who was he?
> Blush, Caledonia! such thy son could be!
> England! I joy no child he was of thine:
> Thy free-born men should spare what once was free;
> Yet they could violate each saddening shrine,
> And bear these altars o'er the long-reluctant brine.
> (I.11)

His anger is obvious here, as elsewhere in the section (11-14), although the subject of it is not entirely clear. After the brief references to "yon fane," Greece almost disappears, returning only when he laments that its citizens were too weak to resist the "robber" (12 and 14). The emphasis seems to be on Elgin, not the removal of the Grecian artifacts. Yet he seems to be as concerned with establishing the role of England in the devastation. First, he takes particular pleasure in the fact that Elgin is not a native-born Englishman (here and in 12), before owning up to his country's complicity. However, he does this in a stanza which begins, misleadingly: "What! shall it e'er be said by British tongue,/Albion was happy in Athena's tears?" (13). But if his focus is not wholly apparent, another matter is. He believes that if Greece had been left alone, its monuments would have remained intact and untroubled:

> "But most the modern Pict's ignoble boast,
> To rive what Goth, and Turk, and Time hath spar'd..."
> (II.12)

These stanzas follow immediately upon a long meditation on time and decay by the comic voice (2-10), and are in dialogue with it. In place of the narrator's specific allegiances (Elgin, England, Greece), this other voice establishes a vision of decline and loss, for which they are no more than the occasion. His Greece is also in ruins, its great men, its "grand in soul," now "Gone--glimmering through the dream (Byron's first manuscript reads, "mingled with the wreck") of things that were" (2). But he sees no other fate for any form or system. He begins by examining the ruins of Athena's temple:

> "Son of the Morning, rise! approach you here!
> Come--but molest not yon defenceless urn:
> Look on this spot--a nation's sepulchre!
> Abode of gods, whose shrines no longer burn."
> (3)

Dazzlingly, he compresses this image and addresses another "temple," a human skull:

> "Look on its broken arch, its ruin'd wall,
> Its chambers desolate, and portals foul:
> Yes, this was once Ambition's airy hall,
> The dome of Thought, the palace of the Soul:
> Behold through each lack-lustre, eyeless hole,
> The gay recess of Wisdom and of Wit
> And Passion's host, that never brook'd control:
> Can all, saint, sage, or sophist ever writ,
> People this lonely tower, this tenement refit?"
> (6)

Drawing upon <u>Hamlet</u>, <u>As You Like It</u> (1.5), and <u>Richard II</u> (1.9), he sketches a world where waste and "wreck" are the natural order. Before such irresistable decay the narrator's loud patiotism or his animated appeals to the citizens of Greece to resist are laughably irrelevant. The comic voice places the despoiled shrines within a temporal scheme that is incompatible with the narrator's immediate and topical frame of reference. These lines anticipate the "Titan's breakfast" passage in <u>Don Juan</u> (14. 1-3):

> "Even gods must yield--religions take their turn:
> 'Twas Jove's--'tis Mahomet's--and other creeds
> Will rise with other years, till man shall learn
> Vainly his incense soars, his victim bleeds;
> Poor Child of Doubt and Death, whose hope is built on reeds."
> (3)

So powerful is this cycle, so pervasive are its ruins, that what it wastes cannot be "restored" even by the imagination:

> "Here let me sit upon this massy stone,
> The marble column's yet unshaken base;
> Here, son of Saturn! was thy fav'rite throne:
> Mightiest of many such! Hence let me trace
> The latent grandeur of thy dwelling place.
> It may not be: nor ev'n can Fancy's eye
> Restore what Time hath labour'd to deface.
> Yet these proud pillars claim no passing sigh,
> Unmov'd the Moslem sits, the light Greek carols by."
> (10)

The narrator's stanzas on Elgin immediately follow these lines. Once again he has been betrayed by a context, and his comments--especially his confident claim, "and Time hath spar'd"--proceed in the accents of unsuspecting parody.

Cantos I and II of <u>Childe Harold</u> have been fashioned from many such dialogues between the narrator and what I have been calling the comic voice. The latter frequently serves as a kind of check upon the former's rhetoric, and interrupts him when he has spoken too casually, or without thinking through what he is saying. For instance, the narrator makes a number of incidental, deprecating remarks about poetry in the course of the poem. Referring to the Portugese coast, he writes, "Which poets vainly pave with sands of gold" (I.16). The variants in the manuscript are instructive here; Byron wrote, "Which poets, prone to lie...," "Which poets sprinkle o'er...," and "Which fabling poets...," before arriving at a final version. Or he introduces Cintra in this fashion:

> "Lo! Cintra's glorious Eden intervenes
> In variegated maze of mount and glen.
> Ah, me! what hand can pencil guide, or pen,
> To follow half on which the eye dilates
> Through views more dazzling unto mortal ken
> Than those whereof such things the bard relates,
> Who to the awe-struck world unlock'd Elysium's gates?
> (I.18)

The reference in the final lines is to Paradise Lost (IV.131ff.). During the next stanza, in imitation of Milton's catalogue, he presents a list of Cintra's Edenic qualities.

Later in the same Canto he again combines a criticism of poetry with the creation of a modern paradise. In form it hovers between a taunt and a rhetorical question:

> "Match me, ye climes! which poets love to laud;
> Match me, ye harams of the land! where now
> I strike my strain, far distant, to applaud
> Beauties that ev'n a cynic must avow;
> Match me those Houries, whom ye scarce allow
> To taste the gale lest Love should ride the wind,
> With Spain's dark-glancing daughters--deign to know,
> There your wise Prophet's paradise we find,
> His black-eyed maids of Heaven, angelically kind.
> (I.59)

This time the comic voice does not allow the narrator's language to pass without comment. Though no answer was anticipated, he breaks into the poem with a response that occupies four stanzas. Speaking in the guise of one of the narrator's "poets," he begins:

> "Oh, thou Parnassus! whom I now survey,
> Not in the phrenzy of a dreamer's eye,
> Not in the fabled landscape of a lay,
> But soaring snow-clad through thy native sky,
> In the wild pomp of mountain majesty!
> What marvel if I thus essay to sing?
> The humblest of thy pilgrims passing by

>   Would gladly woo thine Echoes with his string,
>   Though from thy heights no more one Muse will wave
>   her wing."
>   (I.60)

This is a violent disruption of the poem both chronologically and spatially. In "matching" Spain with Parnassus, the comic voice is making an extreme but perfect gesture which has implications for both paradises and poetry. Where the narrator was casual and ecstatic, he is exacting, serious and melancholy. He turns the former's rhetoric back on him. The narrator wrote, "I strike my strain, far distant, to applaud"; but the comic voice carefully points out that he is in the midst of what he is describing: "Oh, thou Parnassus! whom I <u>now</u> survey..."; and more precisely--

>   "Happier in this than mightiest bards have been,
>   Whose fate <u>to</u> <u>distant</u> homes confin'd their lot,
>   Shall I unmov'd behold the hallow'd scene,
>   Which others rave of, though they know it not?"
>   (62)

Against the narrator's conception of poets as "fabling" and "prone to lie," he insists upon the physical presence of Parnassus: "oft have I dream'd of Thee" (61), he notes, but now he views the mountain "Not in the phrenzy of a dreamer's eye,/Not in the fabled landscape of a lay,/But soaring snow-clad through thy native sky..." The comic voice is unremittingly serious about poetry. He admits to doubts about his ability to find words for what he is experiencing at Parnassus,

>   "And now I view thee, 'tis, alas! with shame
>   That I in feeblest accents must adore.
>   When I recount thy worshippers of yore
>   I tremble, and can only bend the knee;"
>   (61)

--even as he expresses a desire for some future literary fame:

> "...but from thy holy haunt
> Let me some remnant, some memorial bear;
> Yield me one leaf of Daphne's deathless plant,
> Nor let thy votary's hope be deem'd an idle vaunt."

And despite the narrator's caution before poets and poetry, the comic voice is much more scrupulous about his own fictions and mythologies. One sign of this is his refusal to approach Parnassus in a spirit of nostalgia or to claim it as a paradise. Instead, he attends to its physical and spiritual ruin:

> "Though from thy heights no more one Muse will wave
> her wing."
> (60)

> "Though here no more Apollo haunts his grot,
> And thou, the Muses' seat, art now their grave,"
> (62)

He has called upon Parnassus not just as a symbol of "man's divinest love" (61), but precisely because it is a paradise in ruins. He responds to the narrator's appropriation of Cintra and Spain as new Edens by pointing to the fate of one of the most sublime and heralded of all paradises. At this point the narrator's situation is precisely the opposite of what he conceives it to be. In his nonchalant mythologizing it is he, not the poet, who is "fabling" and "prone to lie." The section ends with a playful tug of war between the narrator and the comic voice for control of the poem:

> "Of thee hereafter.--Ev'n amidst my strain
> I turn'd aside to pay my homage here;
> Forgot the land, the sons, the maids of Spain;
> Her fate, to every freeborn bosom dear,
> And hail'd thee, not perchance without a tear.

>   Now to my theme--but from thy holy haunt
>   Let me some remnant, some memorial bear;
>   Yield me one leaf of Daphne's deathless plant,
>   Nor let thy votary's hope be deem'd an idle vaunt."
>   (63)

Then the narrator takes over, and Parnassus becomes just one more figure of speech: "But ne'er didst thou, fair Mount! when Greece was young...Behold a train more fitting to inspire/The song of love, than Andalusia's maids..." (64).

On other occasions the interaction of the narrator and the comic voice is even more dramatic. In a section on the Spanish struggle for independence (I.34-45) they "debate" issues of war, time, and poetry. The narrator speaks first:

>   "But ere the mingling bounds have far been pass'd
>   Dark Guadiana rolls his power along
>   In sullen billows, murmuring and vast,
>   So noted ancient roundelays among.
>   Whilome upon his banks did legions throng
>   Of Moor and knight, in mailed splendour drest:
>   Here ceas'd the swift their race, here sunk the
>   strong;
>   The Paynim turban and the Christian crest
>   Mix'd on the bleeding stream, by floating hosts
>   oppress'd.
>   (34)

He begins by invoking and praising an earlier age of Spanish Chivalry, supporting his attitude by means of antique diction, references to certain stock figures from the period ("Of Moor and Knight, in mailed splendour dressed") and the authority of "noted ancient roundelays." His temperament is entirely classical; he turns to models from the past for guidance in the present. He even makes an allusion to one of the most "noted ancient" texts of all, The Aeneid. The last line echoes "...ubi tot Simoe's correpta sub undis/ scuta virum galeasque et fortia corpora voluit!" (I.11.100-1).

Here, and again in stanza 37 (which also draws upon <u>The Aeneid</u>, I.1.198ff.), where he writes,

> "Awake, ye sons of Spain! awake! advance!
> Lo! Chivalry, your ancient goddess, cries...
> In every peal she calls--'Awake! arise!'
> Say, is her voice more feeble than of yore,
> When her war-song was heard on Andalusia's shore?"

he turns the Spaniards into modern versions of Aeneas and his followers, and urges them to fight and restore former glory.

The comic voice, who has a very different sense of the usefulness of literature and the value of the heroic tradition, counters the narrator's efforts to recreate the exploits of earlier valiants. He turns to the same "roundelays" and epics:

> "Teems not each ditty with the glorious tale?
> Ah! such, alas! the hero's amplest fate!
> When granite moulders and when records fail,
> A peasant's plaint prolongs his dubious date.
> Pride! bend thine eye from heaven to thine estate;
> See how the Mighty shrink into a song!
> Can Volume, Pillar, Pile preserve thee great?
> Or must thou trust Tradition's simple tongue,
> When Flattery sleeps with thee, and History does thee wrong?"
>   (36)

The lines question both the heroic posture that the narrator has been promoting and the means (epics, histories, records, memorials, and oral tradition) by which all achievements are chronicled and passed down. He draws attention to the conditions that render accurate remembrance spectacularly improbable (ll.3-4 and 8-9), and has a more than Horatian gloom about the prospects for immortality. The idea is not so much that daring activities will be distorted and overwhelmed by the passage of time; but are they worth considering at all--"Teems not each ditty with the glorious tale?/ Ah! such, alas! the hero's amplest fate!" The allusion to the <u>Second Book of Samuel</u> (1.7) is a burlesque on the narrator's reliance in this section on Biblical citations (in 33, 38, and 39).

The exchanges between the two voices here are so immediate and pointed that their dialogue takes on some of the qualities of stichomythia, though the argument is conducted in stanzas not individual lines. When the narrator portrays war in vivid, highly visual images,

> "Lo! where the Giant on the mountain stands,
> His blood-red tresses deep'ning in the sun,
> With death-shot glowing in his fiery hands,
> And eye that scorcheth all it glares upon;
> Restless it rolls, now fix'd, and now anon
> Flashing afar,--and at his iron feet
> Destruction cowers to mark what deeds are done;
> For on this morn three potent nations meet,
> To shed before his shrine the blood he deems most sweet."
> (39)

the comic voice directly parries with this:

> "By Heaven! it is a splendid sight to see
> (For one who hath no friend, no brother there)
> Their rival scarfs of mix'd embroidery,
> Their various arms that glitter in the air!
> What gallant war-hounds rouse them from their lair,
> And gnash their fangs, loud yelling for the prey!
> All join the chase, but few the triumph share;
> The Grave shall bear the chiefest prize away,
> And Havoc scarce for joy can number their array."
> (40)

The second stanza sardonically absorbs, and then extends, the assumptions and attitudes of the first; viewed through the lens that the narrator has just provided, battle is indeed "a splendid sight to see." But in a sly parenthesis, the comic voice suggests that war has consequences that are not exclusively aesthetic. His final couplet, itself a travesty of the narrator's inclination to direct the poem toward mythology and allegory ("Lo! where the Giant on the mountain stands..."; "Death rides upon the sulphury Siroc,/Red Battle stamps his foot..." in 38), penetrates the "glitter" and the "mixed embroidery": "The Grave shall bear the Chiefest prize away,/And Havoc scarce for joy can number their array."

After this the comic voice offers the first of a pair of "answers" to the narrator's application of The Aeneid. He comments upon the presence of French and British soldiers in Spain, who--like Aeneas--left home to risk death:

> "The shouts are France, Spain, Albion, Victory!
> The foe, the victim, and the fond ally
> That fights for all, but ever fights in vain,
> Are met--as if at home they could not die--
> To feed the crow on Talavera's plain,
> And fertilize the field that each pretends to gain."
> (41)

The key phrase here, "as if at home they could not die," tears through pretense so directly and simply that it might have come from one of Shakespeare's fools. Appropriately, the comic voice immediately allies himself with the grandest of these figures, and describes the dead in language that draws upon Falstaff's famous speech on "honor":

> "There shall they rot--Ambition's honour'd fools!
> Yes, Honour decks the turf that wraps their clay!
> (42)

The second line also is a wicked distillation of a sentence in Collins's "Ode" ("How sleep the brave")--"There Honour comes a pilgrim grey,/To bless the turf that wraps their clay."

As the comic voice works toward his own "reading" of *The Aeneid*, he pauses to dismiss the conceit that prompted the narrator to cite it in the first place, the eternizing power of poetry (43-44). Finally, he tells us what he has taken away from Virgil's poem:

>"...'Gainst fate to strive
>Where Desolation plants her famish'd brood
>Is vain, or Ilion, Tyre might yet survive,
>And Virtue vanquish all, and Murder cease to thrive."
>(45)

The idea that is is foolish to fight against fate has actually been present in the section from the very start, though the narrator was unaware of it. Once again he opted for a phrase not a context when he quoted from *The Aeneid*: Aeneas, in a moment of great doubt, is declaring that he cannot go on, and wishes that he had died with Hector and Sarpedon. Also, the Biblical passage that he paraphrases in that stanza ("Here ceas'd the swift their race, here sunk the strong") is from *Ecclesiastes*, and defines the vanity of everything "under the sun": "I returned, and saw under the sun, that the race is not to the swift, nor the battle to the strong, neither yet bread to the wise, nor yet riches to men of understanding, nor yet favour to men of skill; but _time_ _and_ _chance_ _happeneth_ _to_ _them_ _all_" (9:11; my italics).

The stanza in which the comic voice defines his sense of "fate" begins with a mention of Childe Harold: "Full swiftly Harold wends his lovely way/Where proud Sevilla triumphs unsubdued." His isolation and the speed of his departure carry the suggestion that he sympathizes with the comic voice's detachment and indifference here. Harold's relationship with the two main voices in the poem is a complicated one. But as one would expect, he is regularly implicated in the exchanges between the narrator and the comic voice, particularly when the former is urging him along his "pilgrimage." One of the more suggestive instances of this is the "Calypso" or "Florence" episode (II.28-36). On this occasion the narrator is intent on a swift departure of his own, seeking to leave behind a scene of "Meditation" and "Solitude" (22-27) that captivated the comic voice:

> "Pass we the long, unvarying course, the track
> Oft trod, that never leaves a trace behind...
> Pass we the joys and sorrows sailors find,
> Coop'd in their winged sea-girt citadel;
> The foul, the fair, the contrary, the kind,
> As breezes rise and fall and billows swell,
> Till on some jocund morn--lo, land! and all is well."
> (28)

But the comic voice does not let him "pass"; though "land" is near, all is decidedly not well. Harold is sailing by Goza and Maltor, which Byron believed were the islands of Calypso:

> "But not in silence pass Calypso's isles,
> The sister tenants of the middle deep;
> There for the weary still a haven smiles,
> Though the fair goddess long hath ceas'd to weep,
> And o'er her cliffs a fruitless watch to keep
> For him who dar'd prefer a mortal bride:
> Here, too, his boy essay'd the dreadful leap
> Stern Mentor urg'd from high to yonder tide;
> While thus of both bereft, the nymph-queen doubly sigh'd."

He is obviously moved by the associations that the islands have with the <u>Odyssey</u> (1.1-6) and with Fénelon's popular imitation and sequel, <u>Télémaque</u> (11.8-9). He resists the narrator's "silence," and locates a rather different resting place (1.3) from the one that earlier had been desired for Harold.

In the next stanza, the narrator attempts to deprecate the spirit of the place and alter the mood. He writes, "Her reign is past, her gentle glories gone." He then offers Harold the first of two lessons about love:

>   ...too easy youth, beware!
>   A mortal sovereign holds her dangerous throne,
>   And thou may'st find a new Calypso there."
>   (30)

His warning, like his descriptions of Harold that I discussed earlier, should give us pause. Nowhere in the poem, either in the narrator's or his own words, does the Childe behave in a manner that might justify the words, "too easy youth." In fact, isn't he anything but "at ease," "free from care," "credulous," or "naive"? The speech that the narrator ascribes to Harold ("Thus Harold deem'd") is also suspect.

>   "Sweet Florence! could another ever share
>   This wayward, loveless heart, it would be thine:
>   But check'd by every tie, I may not dare
>   To cast a worthless offering at thy shrine,
>   Nor ask so dear a breast to feel one pang for mine."
>   (30)

The love that Florence offers is different from any form of that emotion that is connected with Harold in the poem. For her love is a kind of ritualized game, a dramatic interlude with no serious consequences:

>   "Fair Florence found, in sooth with some amaze,
>   One who, 'twas said, still sigh'd to all he saw,
>   Withstand, unmov'd, the lustre of her gaze,
>   Which others hail'd with real, or mimic awe,

>   Their hope, their doom, their punishment, their law;
>   All that gay Beauty from her bondsmen claims:
>   And much she marvell'd that a youth so raw
>   Nor felt, nor feign'd at least, the oft-told flames,
>   Which, though sometimes they frown, yet rarely anger
>   dames."
>
>   (32)

Whether love is "felt" or "feign'd," "real" or "mimic" does not concern her; "frowns" do not really connote "anger," they are only strategies; joining in the dance is all that matters--"All that gay Beauty from her bondsmen claims." In her lack of knowledge of Harold ("'twas said") she resembles the narrator. It is not surprising, then, that he shares her view of love. He regards the Childe as just another player or actor, and refers to his "seeming marble-heart,/Now mask'd in silence..." (33). Then he presents his second "lesson," which details some of the strategies which might bring men success in the game.

>   "Not much he kens, I ween, of woman's breast,
>   Who thinks that wanton thing is won by sighs;
>   What careth she for hearts when once possess'd?
>   Do proper homage to thine idol's eyes;
>   But not too humbly, or she will despise
>   Thee and thy suit, though told in moving tropes:
>   Disguise ev'n tenderness, if thou art wise;
>   Brisk Confidence still best with woman copes;
>   Pique her and soothe in turn, soon Passion crowns thy
>   hopes.
>
>   (34)

His assumptions are the same as Florence's: love proceeds by means of "disguises" and tricks. One possesses or is in turn possessed, and there is no more to it than that. At this point the comic voice returns to the poem. He mimics the accents of the narrator--<u>his</u> playful "disguise" now-- before reiterating the tragic vision of love that began the section:

> "'Tis an old lesson; Time approves it true,
> And those who know it best, deplore it most;
> When all is won that all desire to woo,
> The paltry prize is hardly worth the cost:
> Youth wasted, minds degraded, honour lost,
> These are thy fruits, successful Passion! these!
> If, kindly cruel, early Hope is crost,
> Still to the last it rankles, a disease,
> Not to be cur'd when Love itself forgets to please."
> (35)

He links himself with Calypso, Ulysses, and Telemachus. The stanza alludes to the discussion of love and sexual behavior in De Rerum Natura, and especially to "Adde quod absumunt viris pereuntque labore...Labitor interea res, et Babylonica fiunt:/Languent officia, atque aegrotat fama vacillans (IV.1121-1124). In the manuscript the fruits of love are even more bitter; line five begins, "Youth wasted, wretches born..."

The vision of love that the comic voice urges here is associated with Childe Harold throughout the two Cantos. Whereas Florence and the narrator suspect him of scheming and feigning, in his song, "To Inez," he straightforwardly confesses his weariness:

> "It is that weariness which springs
> From all I meet, or hear, or see:
> To me no pleasure Beauty brings;
> Thine eyes have scarce a charm for me."
> (4)

As the comic voice found a "haven" by Calypso's islands, Harold is soothed when he passes "the barren spot/Where sad Penelope o'erlook'd the wave" (II.39), or the rocks from which Sappho leaped to her death:

> "But when he saw the evening star above
> Leucadia's far-projecting rock of woe,
> And hail'd the last resort of fruitless love,
> He felt, or deem'd he felt, no common glow:

> And as the stately vessel glided slow
> Beneath the shadow of that ancient mount,
> He watch'd the billows' melancholy flow,
> And, sunk albeit in thought as he was wont,
> More placid seem'd his eye, and smooth his pallid front."
> (II.41)

It is by means of what Jerome McGann calls Byron's "uncanny knack for quotation"[6] that the comic voice's vision of love and Harold's finally become indistinguishable. The final lines of this stanza glance at the same section of Lucretius's poem that I excerpted earlier:

> "Oh! many a time, and oft, had Harold lov'd,
> Or dream'd he lov'd, since Rapture is a dream;
> But now his wayward bosom was unmov'd,
> For not yet had he drunk of Lethe's stream;
> And lately had he learn'd with truth to deem
> Love has no gift so grateful as his wings:
> How fair, how young, how soft soe'er he seem,
> Full from the fount of Joy'd delicious springs
> Some bitter o'er the flowers its bubbling venom flings."
> (I.82)

As the "Calypso" section draws to a close, it is the comic voice that has the last word. Again, he imitates the narrator's tone and posture, dismissing the idea of "lessons" almost altogether: "Away! nor let me loiter in my song,/For we have many a mountain-path to tread...To teach man what he might be, or he ought;/If that corrupted thing could ever such be taught."(36)

On only one other occasion does the narrator conclude a passage by attributing it retrospectively to Childe Harold. The section on the Convention of Cintra anticipates, and strictly parallels the "Calypso" episode. Here is the last of three stanzas (I.24-26) which, by means of a similar formula, "So deemed the Childe," ostensibly have Harold as their speaker:

> "And ever since that martial synod met,
> Britannia sickens, Cintra! at thy name;
> And folks in office at the mention fret,
> And fain would blush, if blush they could, for shame.
> How will posterity the deed proclaim!
> Will not our own and fellow-nations sneer,
> To view these champions cheated of their fame,
> By foes in fight o'erthrown, yet victors here,
> Where Scorn her fingers points through many a coming year?"
>
> (26)

The fussiness about "Posterity" and "fame" already has been put in perspective by the comic voice; he ends the segment which immediately precedes this: "how/Vain are the pleasures on earth supplied,/Swept into wrecks anon by Time's ungentle tide!" (23). But much more pertinently, the narrator's claim that the sentiments are Harold's is instantly belied by his activities in the rest of the stanza:

> "So deem'd the Childe, as o'er the mountains he
> Did take his way in solitary guise:
> Sweet was the scene, yet soon he thought to flee,
> More restless than the swallow in the skies:
> Though here awhile he learn'd to moralize,
> For Meditation fix'd at times on him;
> And conscious Reason whisper'd to despise
> His early youth, mispent in maddest whim;
> But as he gaz'd on truth his aching eyes grew dim."
>
> (27)

Despite the assertion that "here awhile he learn'd to moralize," all of his actions intimate otherwise--"yet soon he thought to flee," and "as he gaz'd on truth his aching eyes grew dim." These phrases resemble the description of his departure from Spain ("Full swiftly Harold wends his lonely way...") and, once again, suggest aloofness, indifference, and perhaps even boredom. Here, as in Spain, he seems to be thinking only of a quick exit from the scene; and that is just what happens: "To horse! to horse! he quits, for ever quits/A scene of peace, though soothing to his soul..." (28).

Moreover, there are no other instances in the poem where Harold voices or is allied with the opinions that the narrator ascribes to him here. Each time the subject is some aspect of war, his attitude accords with the position of the comic voice that I examined earlier. In contrast to the narrator's excitement and animation, Childe Harold is uninterested and scoffing:

> "Oft did he mark the scenes of vanish'd war,
> Actium, Lepanto, fatal Trafalgar;
> Mark them unmov'd, for he would not delight...
> In themes of bloody fray, or gallant fight,
> But loath'd the bravo's trade, and laugh'd at martial wight."
>
> (II.40)

Or after the narrator wonders why the citizens of Greece do not rise up against those who, like Elgin, are robbing them, he identifies himself with their cause in the most intimate terms: "Cold is the heart, fair Greece! that looks on thee,/Nor feels as lovers o'er the dust they lov'd"(II.15). In the very next stanza Harold joins the ranks of the "cold" of heart.

> "... the cold stranger pass'd to other climes:
> Hard is the heart whom charms may not enslave;
> But Harold felt not as in other times,
> And left without a sigh the land of war and crimes."
>
> (16)

It is the narrator, then, who is so pained and incensed by the Convention of Cintra. His fascination with the materials of war and battle is so pervasive that it does not need the prompting of a specific political situation like Cintra, Spain, or Greece. The bustle about Harold's ship as it sets sail is enough to summon its phrases: "And oh!, the little warlike world within!/The well-reev'd guns, the netted canopy,/The hoarse command, the busy humming din,/When, at a word, the tops are mann'd on high..." (18).

The "Calypso" interlude and these stanzas on Cintra are part of the narrator's efforts to shape the various occurences along Harold's journey into an organically developing "pilgrimage." His guiding hand, directing the Childe toward the goals of "rest" and insight--here, for instance, proposing "attributions" that cannot be distinguished from impositions and intrusions--, can be observed throughout the poem, as I argued earlier; but his presence is discernible more often, and is more intensely felt, in the second Canto. By the middle of that Canto, we find him working to secure what only can be termed "a happy ending" for Harold and for Childe Harold's Pilgrimage.

Cintra and "Calypso" are mirror images of these later, more emphatic and palpable instances of what James Merrill, speaking of his difficulties in organizing his long poem Mirabell, calls "blunt stabs at 'design.'"[7] The narrator will place Harold in a setting conducive to "peace" or in circumstances appropriate for "reflection" and instruction, only to have his best intentions counteracted by some other strain in the poem, associated with the comic voice or Harold, or a wayward impulse in his own rhetoric. Shortly after leaving Malta and Leucadia, Harold arrives in Albania. There the narrator fashions a third paradise for him:

> "Here in the sultriest season let him rest,
> Fresh is the green beneath those aged trees;
> Here winds of gentlest wing will fan his breast,
> From heaven itself he may inhale the breeze:
> The plain is far beneath--oh! let him seize
> Pure pleasure while he can; the scorching ray
> Here pierceth not, impregnate with disease:
> Then let his length the loitering pilgrim lay,
> And gaze, untir'd, the morn, the noon, the eve away."
> (50)

Once more the "pilgrim" has reached a haven of "rest" and shelter. The place is openly compared to "Heaven" (1.4); it also resembles Arden in *As You Like It* (lines 6-7 recall Duke Senior's speech, "Here we feel not the penalty of Adam,/The seasons' difference..."). Nothing seems to be wanting here, and the narrator does not want Harold to leave: "Then let his length the loitering pilgrim lay,/And gaze, untir'd..." Yet his depiction of paradise contains the very means of its dissolution. Unlike Arden, and perhaps Heaven, Albania is subject to the passage of time, and his sounding of the *carpe diem* theme--"Oh! let him seize/Pure pleasure while he can"--almost overwhelms the blissful setting, and underscores its inherent fragility.

This note of uneasiness--a clock ticking away in paradise--is amplified in the succeeding stanzas. His confident prescriptions ("let him rest...let (him) lay...") disappear, as does any clear sense of where he is. He has difficulty focusing on what is before him. If the mountains are inarguably, though vaguely, "Dusky and huge," they are also "enlarging on the sight" (51.1.1); if they "extend from right to left" (note how he transfers a feature of his own vision to the mountains), still "a living valley *seems* to stir" beneath them (1.4). The view will not stay put; it is in continuous motion, changes shape, and is not what it first appears to be. It is perhaps like scenery for a play--"Nature's volcanic amphitheatre" (1.2). Paradise even contains a river named Acheron (1.6), a fact which leads the narrator to make a joke: "Pluto! if this be Hell I look upon,/Close sham'd Elysium's gates, my shade shall seek for none!" (11.8-9). However, while this may not be Hell that he has penetrated, he is increasingly uncertain about precisely what it is. He then decides to define the scene in terms of what it is not:

>"Ne city's towers pollute the lovely view;
>Unseen is Yanina, though not remote,
>Veil'd by the screen of hills: here men are few,
>Scanty the hamlet, rare the lonely cot..."
>(52)

As the stanza trails off into a quiet appreciation of goats, sheep, and shepherds, he seems to have abandoned paradise for a more common and tepid version of pastoral. At this point, the comic voice enters the poem and demonstrates how removed from "Heaven" Harold and his narrator really are.

>"Oh! where, Dodona! is thine aged grove,
>Prophetic fount, and oracle divine?
>What valley echo'd the response of Jove?
>What trace remaineth of the thunderer's shrine?
>All, all forgotten--and shall man repine
>That his frail bonds to fleeting life are broke?
>Cease, fool! the fate of gods may well be thine:
>Wouldst thou survive the marble or the oak?
>When nations, tongues, and worlds must sink beneath the stroke!"
>(53)

The comic voice brusquely dismantles the paradise that the narrator's amiable language invoked, and marks it as a witless indulgence ("Cease, fool!"). Time's gentle nudge

in stanza 50 returns as a violent explosion, wrecking the
promised peace and rest. Like the ruins at Parnassus, the
destruction of Dodona locates the narrator's quest within a
comprehensive perspective, and serves as a bleak reminder of
the destiny of other paradises and pilgrimages. After this
fierce outburst, the comic voice once more, but lightly and
playfully now, mimics the narrator, dallying with his vision
of the "untir'd" pilgrim, soothed and sustained by the mountain scenery. He also reproduces a bit of his antique diction.

> "Epirus' bounds recede, and mountains fail;
> Tir'd of up-gazing still, the wearied eye
> Reposes gladly on as smooth a vale
> As even Spring yclad in grassy dye..."
> (54)

Naturally, the narrator's teleological inclinations are
most visible in the final episodes of the poem. Now and then
his efforts will be unnerved and thwarted--these lines, for
instance, reenact in miniature the drama of rest and weariness that I have just depicted:

> "'Mid many things most new to ear and eye
> The pilgrim rested here his weary feet,
> And gaz'd around on Moslem luxury
> Till quickly wearied with that spacious seat..."
> (64)

But this is rare; and he carries on otherwise unobstructed
until the last few stanzas. Yet the signs of his shaping
presence, guiding Harold (and the poem) toward his goal,
are everywhere. In the repetition of phrases like "It chanc'd
that (67), and "It came to pass" (69) we can hear the busy
storyteller prodding and steering his materials to a particular end. And his manipulation of the last two sequences--

Harold's visit with Ali Pasha in Albania, and the arrival in Greece--is more self-consciously didactic than at any other point in <u>Childe Harold</u>. Each episode is structured as a series of lessons; when Harold has passed through them his "pilgrimage," in the narrator's scheme of things, is complete.

In Albania Harold's education primarily proceeds by means of the unanticipated acts of kindness that he witnesses and benefits from there. On three occasions ("It came to pass" has religious as well as narrative significance) he is helped and cared for by people he had previously imagined as savage and barbaric. The situations are exactly parallel. In each fear and suspicion give way to relief and friendship. When he first sees the Albanians "in their Chieftain's tower/Thronging to war in splendour and success" he believes that his life is in danger:

> "But these did shelter him beneath their roof,
> When less barbarians would have cheered him less,
> And fellow-countrymen have stood aloof--
> In aught that tries the heart how few withstand the proof!"
>
> (66)

There was in fact no threat at all. From the Albanians he receives not only shelter, but instruction in the nature of appearance and of friendship. Later, his ship is lost, and again he fears for his life.

> "Vain fear! the Suliotes stretch'd the welcome hand,
> Led them o'er rocks and past the dangerous swamp,
> Kinder than polish'd slaves though not so bland,
> And pil'd the hearth, and wrung their garments damp,
> And fill'd the bowl, and trimm'd the cheerful lamp,
> And spread their fare; though homely, all they had:
> Such conduct bears Philanthropy's rare stamp--

> To rest the weary and to soothe the sad,
> Doth lesson happier men, and shames at least the bad."
> (68)

This stanza, more forcibly than the previous one I quoted, bears the narrator's own "rare stamp." The final lines, in particular, virtually restate the definition of "pilgrimage" that he offered in the previous Canto (28). If "such conduct" can "rest the weary," "soothe the sad," and "lesson ...men," Harold's journey must be almost over. And the third generous action does lead to some form of resolution. After "marauders" block his path, a "trusty band" of Albanians leads him to safety (69). There for the first time in the poem he joins a human community: "Here Harold was receiv'd a welcome guest;/Nor did he pass unmov'd the gentle scene,/For many a joy could he from Night's soft presence glean" (70).

One feature of the "gentle scene" is a feast, with drinking, singing, and dancing. The narrator describes the evening this way:

> "Childe Harold at a little distance stood
> And view'd, but not displeas'd, the revelrie,
> Nor hated harmless mirth, however rude:
> In sooth, it was no vulgar sight to see
> Their barbarous, yet their not indecent, glee,
> And, as the flames along their faces gleam'd,
> Their gestures nimble, dark eyes flashing free,
> The long wild locks that to their girdles stream'd,
> While thus in concert they this lay half sang, half scream'd."
> (72)

This is followed by an English "translation" of an Albanian song.

There are more than a few curious and suspicious elements in this account of Harold's evolution. He is almost entirely absent from it, at least as a thinking, speaking presence; his response to Albania is not in the poem. The language in which all the events have been depicted is entirely the narrator's, not just "rest," "soothe," "lesson," and "shames," but less obvious words like "vulgar" (see I.5, 79, and II.88) or "rude" (see I.14, 85, and II.49). Moreover, only the last of the lessons is directly connected to Harold; the others remain unfocused abstractions with no particular references (in this they resemble many of the narrator's earlier descriptions of Harold--I.3 or I.10, for instance). And the claims of the third are extremely weak: "Nor did he pass unmov'd," and "Harold at a little distance stood/And view'd, but not displeas'd..." Then there is the question of what is being solemnized here. If the "gentle scene" is a feast, it is also a celebration of war, revenge, robbery, and casual slaughter. In its savagery, the Albanian song surpasses anything else in the poem--the bullfight or the Spanish wars.

>   "Tambourgi! Tambourgi! thy 'larum afar
>   Gives hope to the valiant, and promise of war;
>   All the sons of the mountains arise at the note,
>   Chimariot, Illyrian, and dark Suliote!
>
>   . . .
>
>   Macedonia sends forth her invincible race;
>   For a time they abandon the cave and the chase:
>   But those scarfs of blood-red shall be redder, before
>   The sabre is sheath'd and the battle is o'er.
>
>   . . .
>
>   Remember the moment when Previsa fell,
>   The shrieks of the conquer'd, the conquerors' yell;
>   The roofs that we fir'd, and the plunder we shar'd,
>   The wealthy we slaughter'd, the lovely we spar'd.

> I talk not of mercy, I talk not of fear;
> He neither must know who would serve the Vizier:
> Since the days of our prophet the Crescent ne'er saw
> A chief ever glorious like Ali Pashaw."
> (1, 4, 8, 9)

Love was only a kind of mock war in Cadiz and London, and feeble competition with this:

> "I ask not the pleasures that riches supply,
> My sabre shall win what the feeble must buy;
> Shall win the young bride with her long flowing hair,
> And many a maid from her mother shall tear.
>
> I love the fair face of the maid in her youth,
> Her caresses shall lull me, her music shall sooth;
> Let her bring from the chamber her many-ton'd lyre,
> And sing us a song on the fall of her sire."
> (6-7)

"Tambourgi! Tambourgi!" is a virtual compendium of everything Harold abhors or is indifferent to; such odd circumstances for what is supposedly the penultimate stage of his "pilgrimage."

The resolution that the narrator effects here is, of course, a formal one only. The Albanian episode is the most extreme example in the poem of his failure to attend to the implications and contexts of what he is saying. He pushes on, captivated by the *idée fixe* of a "pilgrimage," and seems not to notice that every aspect of the scene is resisting him, and that his vision of Harold's journey is collapsing around him. In his single-mindedness, despite all the surrounding conditions, he resembles Buster Keaton in James Agee's famous description:

> "Trapped in the side wheel of a ferry-boat, saving himself from drowning only by walking, then desperately running, inside the accelerating wheel like a squirrel in a cage, his only real concern was, obviously, to keep his hat on."[8]

He is so intent on bringing the story to a fortunate conclusion that he is willing to drop Harold from the poem in order to accomplish this. Not only is Harold silent after the Albanian war-song; he also disappears, not to reemerge in the Canto.

The sentiments on war and love that are expressed in "Tambourgi! Tambourgi!" are an extreme version of the narrator's, though on no occasion does he ever approximate its ferocity. However, he did approve of the Albanians from the very start:

> "Fierce are Albania's children, yet they lack
> Not virtues, were those virtues more mature.
> Where is the foe that ever saw their back?
> Who can so well the toil of war endure?
> Their native fastnesses not more secure
> Than they in doubtful time of troublous need:
> Their wrath how deadly! but their friendship sure,
> When Gratitude or Valour bids them bleed,
> Unshaken rushing on where'er their chief may lead."
> (65)

And if Harold is suspicious of the Albanians, and is surprised by the kindness that waits beneath their fierce demeanors, the narrator has to remind himself that they can be dangerous.

> "Ali reclin'd, a man of war and woes;
> Yet in his lineaments ye cannot trace,
> While Gentleness her milder radiance throws
> Along that aged venerable face,
> The deeds that lurk beneath, and stain him with disgrace."
> (62)

In the end, it is he who responds to the martial strains of the Albanian song. Immediately upon its close--"view us as victors, or view us no more!"--he summons the citizens of Greece to war:

> "Fair Greece! sad relic of departed worth!
> Immortal, though no more! though fallen, great!
> Who now shall lead thy scatter'd children forth,
> And long accustom'd bondage uncreate?
> Not such thy sons who whilome did await,
> The hopeless warriors of a willing doom,
> In bleak Thermopylae's sepulchral strait--
> Oh! who that gallant spirit shall resume,
> Leap from Eurotas' banks, and call thee from the tomb?"
>
> (73)

Greece is the final source of instruction in the Canto, and is where the "pilgrimage," now missing Harold, of course, terminates. What Greece symbolizes for the narrator is not always readily distinguished. Beside the precise applications that the comic voice made of the country and its monuments--Parnassus, the temples of Athen , and Jupiter, Dodona, etc.--his references and reflections are disquietingly unfocused and, at times, contradictory. Though he calls the Greeks to battle here (and more enthusiastically in 76), he soon shapes an <u>adjunata</u>, or list of impossibilities, to demonstrate that they will never be victorious:

> "When riseth Lacedemon's hardihood,
> When Thebes Epamenondas rears again,
> When Athens' children are with hearts endued,
> When Grecian mothers shall give birth to men,
> Then may'st thou be restored; but not till then."
>
> (84)

Later, its vanquished state seems to be one source of his pleasure. He writes, "And yet how lovely in thine age of woe,/Land of lost gods and godlike men! art thou!... Thy fanes, thy temples, to thy surface bow,/Commingling slowly with heroic earth,/Broke by the share of every rustic plough..." (85).

His attitude toward the citizens of Greece is no less

ambivalent. With great bitterness he attacks those who indulge in the pre-Lenten celebrations while they are not free from Turkish domination:

> "But, midst the throng in merry masquerade,
> Lurk there no hearts that throb with secret pain,
> Even through the closest searment half betrayed?
>
> . . .
>
> This must he feel, the true-born son of Greece,
> If Greece one true-born patriot still can boast...
> Ah! Greece! they love these least who owe thee most;
> Their birth, their blood, and that sublime record
> Of hero sires, who shame thy now degenerate horde."
> (82-83)

And he celebrates the revellers:

> "Glane's many a light caique along the foam,
> Danc'd on the shore the daughters of the land,
> Ne thought had man or maid of rest or home,
> While many a languid eye and thrilling hand
> Exchang'd the look few bosoms may withstand,
> Or gently prest, return'd the pressure still:
> Oh Love! young Love! bound in thy rosy band,
> Let sage or cynic prattle as he will,
> These hours, and only these, redeem Life's years of
>   ill!"
> (81)

There are small attendant perplexities as well. For instance, at one point he draws upon Horace (IV.ix.25ff) and the <u>Book of Ecclesiasticus</u> (44.8-9) to suggest (as in the "Sons of Spain" passage) the eternizing powers of poetry and art: "So perish monuments of mortal birth/So perish all in turn, save well-recorded Worth" (85); but when we turn the page we learn that, "Yet are thy skies as blue, thy crags as wild... Art, Glory, Freedom fail, but Nature still is fair" (87). Though not even nature emerges untarnished: "Couldst thou forebode the dismal hour which now/Dims the green beauties of thine Attic plain?" (74).

In spite of these irreconcilable attitudes and tones, and the confused, fluctuating conception of Greece that is offered here, there is one steady pulse that beats through these stanzas: the narrator's assertion that Greece is a "holy" and "magic" place. These words, or variations on them ("realm of wonder," "hallowed ground," "sacred," and "consecrated land"), advance his vision of the "pilgrimage," even though, as in Albania, the particulars and details of the scene do not coalesce to shape and sustain it. Nevertheless, it is in Greece that he insists on bringing the sojourn to a conclusion:

> "Yet to the remnants of thy splendour past
> Shall pilgrims, pensive, but unwearied, throng;
> Long shall the voyager, with th' Ionian blast,
> Hail the bright clime of battle and of song;
> Long shall thine annals and immortal tongue
> Fill with thy fame the youth of many a shore;
> Boast of the aged! lesson of the young!
> Which sages venerate and bards adore,
> As Pallas and the Muse unveil their awful lore.
>
> The parted bosom clings to wonted home,
> If aught that's kindred cheer the welcome hearth;
> He that is lonely hither let him roam,
> And gaze complacent on congenial earth.
> Greece is no lightsome land of social mirth;
> But he whom Sadness sootheth may abide,
> And scarce regret the region of his birth,
> When wandering slow by Delphi's sacred side,
> Or gazing o'er the plains where Greek and Persian
>   died.
>
> Let such approach this consecrated land,
> And pass in peace along the magic waste..."
>   (91-93)

These lines complete the "pilgrimage" which he promised in the first Canto. He wrote that the journey would be over when "toil his thirst for travel can assuage,/Or he shall calm his heart, or learn experience sage" (I.28). Though his claim is at odds with the uncertain vision of Greece that he has just presented, he declares that all of these conditions have been fulfilled, if not for the absent Harold, at least for a more general class of "pilgrims." His language pointedly realizes his earlier prerequisites (in I.28 and elsewhere): "Shall pilgrims, pensive, but unwearied, throng...," "Boast of the aged! lesson of the young!/Which sages venerate and bards adore...," "He that is lonely hither let him roam/And gaze complacent on congenial earth...," "But he whom Sadness sootheth may abide/And scarce regret the region of his birth...," and, ultimately, "pass in peace along the magic waste." With perhaps even greater exactness, his words satisfy the poem's epigraph, from, Le Cosmopolite:

> "L'univers est use espèce de livre, dont on n'a lu que la première page, quand on n'a vu que son pays. J'en ai feuilleté un assez grand nombre, que j'ai trouvé également mauvaises. Cet examen ne m'a point été infructueux. Je haïssais ma patrie. Toutes les impertinences des peuples divers, parmi lesquels j'ai vécu, m'ont réconcilié avec elle. Quand je n'aurais tiré d'autre bénéfice de mes voyages que celui-là, je n'en regretterais ni les frais, ni les fatigues."

But Childe Harold's Pilgrimage does not, of course, end here. The narrator's carefully wrought and firmly phrased finale is undermined twice before the Canto is finished. He himself weakens the power of his conclusion by going on to trivialize his vision. After the cogent, efficient ring of, "Let such approach this consecrated land/And pass in peace along the magic waste," immediately he sinks to this:

> "But spare its relics--let no busy hand
> Deface the scenes, already how defac'd!
> Not for such purpose were these altars plac'd:
> Revere the remnants nations once rever'd:
> So may our country's name be undisgrac'd,
> So may'st thou prosper where thy youth was rear'd,
> By every honest joy of love and life endear'd."
>
> (93)

The almost chatty tone, the diffuse incidentals and, above all, the narrowness of the concerns ("So may our country's name be undisgrac'd") diminish the forcefulness of the preceding lines, and draw even more attention to their hollowness, and the sense that they do not quite follow from anything he has shown us about Greece. Also, the decline in rhetorical force here recapitulates exactly that moment at the start of the Canto when the comic voice's meditation on the Greek ruins passed to the narrator's attack on Elgin.

Then the comic voice returns to the poem: he began the Canto, and he will end it. He addresses the narrator in a manner that is sarcastic and corrosive:

> "For thee, who thus in too protracted song
> Hast sooth'd thine idlesse with inglorious lays,
> Soon shall thy voice be lost amid the throng
> Of louder minstrels in these later days:
> To such resign the strife for fading bays--
> Ill may such contest now the spirit move
> Which heeds nor keen reproach nor partial praise;
> Since cold each kinder heart that might approve,
> And none are left to please when none are left to
>   love."
>
> (94)

In accents of dazzling, almost giddy bitterness, he compresses and attacks the language of the narrator's conclusion. He conflates "And gaze complacent on congenial earth" and "he whom Sadness sootheth may abide" into "thus in too protracted song/Hast sooth'd thine idlesse." The happy notion, "Long shall the voyager...Hail the bright clime of battle and song" reemerges from his distorting mirror as a spiteful reference to "inglorious lays." The narrator's confident sense of posterity--"Long shall thine annals and immortal tongue/Fill with thy fame the youth of many a shore--becomes a grim prediction: "Soon shall thy voice be lost amid the throng/Of louder minstrels in these later days." And most grievously and poignantly, the warm picture of home amidst genial spirits and sympathy ("The parted bosom clings to wonted home,/If aught that's kindred cheer the welcome hearth..."), returns black and blank: "Since cold each kinder heart that might approve,/And none are left to please when none are left to love."

Just as at the close of the first Canto, the poem is "shocked with a death" that has consequences for both the narrator and the comic voice.[9] Each event fills a corresponding place in its respective Canto. The initial effect in both cases is a denial of the premises which have empowered the narrator's conception of the "pilgrimage," either as it has been in progress (I), or after he has guided it to a conclusion (II). In the first Canto, his final stanzas combining a lament for the Spanish war-dead with criticism of France (85-90), are interrupted by the comic voice in a manner that recalls Harold's "unpremeditated lay" (84; also see 13)--"unavailing woe/Bursts from (his) heart, and mingles with the strain" (91). The occasion, the death of an unnamed friend, prompts him to direct his attention towards the very assumptions the narrator has relied upon to define Harold's sojourn and the poem, and to reject them without ambiguity:[10]

> "Oh, known the earliest and esteem'd the most!
> Dear to a heart where nought was left so dear!
> Though to my hopeless days for ever lost,
> In dreams deny me not to see thee here!
> And Morn in secret shall renew the tear
> Of Consciousness awaking to her woes,
> And Fancy hover o'er thy bloodless bier,
> Till my frail frame return to whence it rose,
> And mourn'd and mourner lie united in repose."
> (I.92)

In his vision of a seemingly unchanging succession of "hopeless days," he dismisses both aspects of the narrator's promised goal. The latter's assurance of insight and knowledge, what he termed "learn experience sage" (I.28), is here rephrased, precisely halfway through the journey, "the tear/Of Consciousness awaking to her woes." The other term of the pledge which underwrote the "pilgrimage," the prospect of "peace" or "rest"--"calm his breast"--is also denied. What the narrator believed would come to Harold at the end of his travels, the comic voice expects to find only in "dreams," in "Fancy" or in the grave: "Till my frail frame return to whence it rose,/And mourn'd and mourner lie united in repose." So sure is he that "repose" is reached only in death, he even expresses his envy of the dead friend--"What hadst thou done to sink so peacefully to rest?" (91).

The perspective at the end of the poem is no less grim; and the second death is also disruptive of the narrator's intentions. The "peace" and sense of reconciliation that the "pilgrims" found in their contact with Greece, its "magic waste," and its historic past has its analogue in the pain the comic voice experiences as he contrasts his personal past with the ruins of his present life. In another instance of "Consciousness awaking to its woes," he writes,

> "Oh! ever loving, lovely, and belov'd!
> How selfish Sorrow ponders on the past,
> And clings to thoughts now better far remov'd!
> But Time shall tear thy shadow from me last.
> All thou could'st have of mine, stern Death! thou hast;
> The parent, friend, and now the more than friend:
> Ne'er yet for one thine arrows flew so fast,
> And grief with grief continuing still to blend,
> Hath snatch'd the little joy that life had yet to lend."
> (96)

And whereas the other "pilgrims" and the narrator have reached the end of their journey, and can return "home," he seems fated to be always on the move:

> "What is my being? thou hast ceas'd to be!
> Nor staid to welcome here thy wanderer home,
> Who mourns o'er hours which we no more shall see--
> Would they had never been, or were to come!
> Would he had ne'er return'd to find fresh cause to roam!"
> (95)

The characterizing term here is "wanderer," not "pilgrim." In contrast with the narrator, the comic voice neither shapes the journey according to a consistent plan nor locates in it any ultimate significance. He is almost entirely without expectations for it. His presence in the poem, as I hope is clear from my discussion of the interaction of the voices, is not so much active and directing as it is reactive and counteractive: he regularly disrupts the narrator's efforts to establish the meaning of Harold's actions and experiences and to structure them systematically. Moreover, it is not only at the end of each Canto that he indicates his distance from the suppositions about the likelihood of knowledge and "peace" that allow the narrator to use the word "pilgrimage." Throughout the poem, but especially in the stanzas that frame the actual journey ("To Ianthe," I.1, II.1-10), he is just as skeptical and pessimistic. These lines in particular, appearing early in the second Canto, effectively counter the narrator's sense of the direction Harold's travels and the poem will take, and the manner in which they will conclude:

> "Well didst thou speak, Athena's wisest son!
> 'All that we know is, nothing can be known.'
> Why should we shrink from what we cannot shun?
> Each has his pang, but feeble sufferers groan
> With brain-born dreams of evil all their own.
> Pursue what Chance or Fate proclaimeth best;
> Peace waits us on the shores of Acheron:
> There no forc'd banquet claims the sated guest,
> But Silence spreads the couch of ever welcome rest."
> (II.7)

The various "goals" that the narrator specified for Harold are redefined as forms of sentimentality. In his insistence upon the possibility of growth through experience, and the prospect of fresh, transfiguring insight, he is "shrink(ing) from what we cannot shun." In place of an all-embracing design, and a teleology, the comic voice urges an undemonstrative perspectivism: "Pursue what Chance or Fate proclaimeth best." And once again, "peace" and "rest" are identified with death.

Harold's own perception of his journey is indistinguishable from that of the comic voice. So disinclined is he to look to his end, that he actually does not seem to care where he is going. For him, the sojourn was begun out of boredom and weariness ("He felt the fulness of satiety...," I.4); if it has a "goal" or purpose, it is diversion and distraction from the tedium and languor of life in his "native Land." The narrator writes disapprovingly of Harold, "With pleasure drugg'd he almost long'd for woe,/And e'en for change of scene would seek the shades below" (I.6). Only a few stanzas later, the Childe echoes this, though without drawing on the narrator's moral and religious language:

> "'With thee, my bark, I'll swiftly go
>   Athwart the foaming brine;
> Nor care what land thou bear'st me to,
>   So not again to mine.
> Welcome, welcome, ye dark-blue waves!
>   And when you fail my sight,
> Welcome, ye deserts, and ye caves!
>   My native Land--Good Night!'"
>
> ("Good night," 10)

Above all else he seeks novelty: "The scene was savage, but the scene was new;/This made the ceaseless toil of travel sweet..." (II.43). His sense of *ennui* rivals Baudelaire's and his expression of it anticipates the conclusion of one of the prose poems in Le Spleen de Paris: "Enfin, mon ame fait explosion, et sagement elle me crie: 'N'importe où! n'importe où! pourvu que ce soit hors de ce monde!'"

His visual response to the narrator's "lessons" is, as I noted earlier, also boredom: "But as he gaz'd on truth his aching eyes grew dim.//To horse! to horse! he quits, for ever quits/A scene of peace, though soothing to his soul..." (I.27-28). When the narrator pauses in the course of the travels to instruct and improve him, Harold is generally impatient to continue and move on: "Full swiftly Harold wends his lonely way" (I.45) or "Harold felt not as in other times/And left without a sigh the land of war and crimes" (II.16). He does not believe that the journey will bring him "peace" or "rest"; like the comic voice he expects this only in the grave:

> "And dost thou ask, what secret woe
> I bear, corroding joy and youth?
> And wilt thou vainly seek to know
> A pang, ev'n thou must fail to soothe?
>
> It is that settled, ceaseless gloom
> The fabled Hebrew wanderer bore;
> That will not look beyond the tomb,
> But cannot hope for rest before."
> ("To Inez," 2 and 5)

In what might be called his epistemology, if his ideas played a more significant role in the drama, he is perhaps even more cynical than the comic voice. The latter is intensely skeptical, and full of doubts, but Harold simply prefers not to know; for him, it seems, only the unexamined life is worth living. He envies the uninformed:

> "Yet others rapt in pleasure seem,
> And taste of all that I forsake;
> Oh! may they still of transport dream,
> And ne'er, at least like me, awake"
> ("To Inez," 7)

And "thought" for him is an enemy:

> "What exile from himself can flee?
> To Zones, though more and more remote,
> Still, still pursues, where-e'er I be,
> The blight of life--the demon, Thought."
> ("To Inez," 6)

Unlike the narrator, who urges the citizens of Spain and Greece to wake up ("Awake, ye sons of Spain!" or "But, midst the throng in merry masquerade,/Lurk there no hearts that throb with secret pain..."), Harold is only reluctantly "awake." He covets the pleasures of the same dreamers and the masked, "feigning" revellers that the narrator castigates and deplores. He has none of Psyche's curiosity, and knows the value of a mask: "Smile on--nor venture to unmask/ Man's heart, and view the Hell that's there" ("To Inez," 9).

A final consequence of the death that is mourned at the conclusion of the second Canto is that it occasions the disappearance of the comic voice--or more precisely, the comic aspects of that voice--from the poem. This is perhaps the most "ruthless" instance of the poem's "contrapuntal technique," and its ultimate evasion of consistency. A good argument can be fashioned to demonstrate that the sorrowful stanzas on time, mortality, and loss at the beginning of the second Canto focus on Greece in order to frame, objectify, and put in perspective the highly personal expression of grief at the end of the previous one. But the second death is accorded no such frame, and the emotions it arouses are not mediated by an appeal to a larger, external scheme. The outermost element in the structure, "To Ianthe," itself a meditation on aging, mortality, and poetry, hints at this; yet the final strains of Childe Harold's Pilgrimage that a Londoner of 1812 would have heard specify implacable, personal woe. At the finish of the journey, what I have been calling the comic voice cannot be distinguished from Childe Harold at the start of his:

>"Then must I plunge again into the crowd,
> And follow all that Peace disdains to seek?
> Where Revel calls, and Laughter, vainly loud,
> False to the heart, distorts the hollow cheek,
> To leave the flagging spirit doubly weak;
> Still o'er the features, which perforce they cheer,
> To feign the pleasure or conceal the pique,
> Smiles form the channel of a future tear,
>Or raise the writhing lip with ill-dissembled sneer.
>
> What is the worst of woes that wait on age?
> What stamps the wrinkle deeper on the brow?
> To view each lov'd one blotted from life's page,
> And be alone on earth, as I am now.
> Before the Chastener humbly let me bow:
> O'er hearts divided and o'er hopes destroy'd,
> Roll on, vain days! full reckless may ye flow,
> Since Time hath reft whate'er my soul enjoy'd,
>And with the ills of Eld mine earlier years alloy'd."
>   (97-98)

The situations are now mirror images of one another. Harold's has also been a comic voice. His response to war and "martial wight" is laughter (II.40). Very early in the poem the narrator identifies him with Touchstone and Jacques in <u>As You Like It</u>:

>"Childe Harold bask'd him in the noon-tide sun,
> Disporting there like any other fly..."
>   (I.4)

And in a conversation with his "staunch yeoman" he defines a comic vision in terms that also draw upon the play:

>"'Come hither, hither, my staunch yeoman,
>   Why dost thou look so pale?
> Or dost thou dread a French foeman?
>   Or shiver at the gale?'--
> 'Deem'st thou I tremble for my life?
>   Sir Childe, I'm not so weak;
> But thinking on an absent wife
>   Will blanch a faithful cheek.
>
> 'My spouse and boys dwell near thy hall,
>   Along the bordering lake,
> And when they on their father call,
>   What answer shall she make?'--
> 'Enough, enough, my yeoman good,
>   Thy grief let none gainsay;

>   But I, who am of lighter mood,
>   Will laugh to flee away.
>
>   'For who would trust the seeming sighs
>   Of wife or paramour?
>   Fresh feres will dry the bright blue eyes
>   We late saw streaming o'er."
>   ("Good night," 6-8)

But his comedy is only an act, his smile only a mask:

>   "Through many a clime 'tis mine to go,
>   With many a retrospection curst;
>   And all my solace is to know,
>   Whate'er betides, I've known the worst.
>
>   What is that worst? Nay do not ask--
>   In pity from the search forbear:
>   Smile on--nor venture to unmask
>   Man's heart, and view the Hell that's there."
>   ("To Inez," 8 and 9)

III

At the Titan's Breakfast

An exemplary feature of Don Juan, and one that is
regularly confused or lost amidst discussions of its auto-
biographic, ethical, or satiric impulses, is the tenacity
with which the languages of the poem refuse to indulge the
notion that there is anything like a raw material for literature, the innocent disclaimer that a life is simpler and
better than our methods and fashions of talking about it.
With an adroitness, range and sophistication comparable to
The Satyricon, Don Quixote, Tristram Shandy, Marvell's
poems and to only the most ambitious undertakings in recent
fiction and poetry, the narrators of Don Juan almost never
present their subjects except as part of the evaluative,
historical, and epistemological interpretations that have
been and might be made of them. In doing so, they typically bring to their task the analytic skills, attitudes and
information that, normally, readers are expected to supply;
and there is a sense in which the poem imparts and directs--
indeed contains--its own best and most exacting criticism.

Inevitably, this criticism is concerned with matters
of literary and personal style. In Don Juan Byron, through
careful acts of rendition and dramatization, attends to the
forces and energies at work in any effort to invest an idea
with a style. Imitating, in turn, the linguistic and conceptual resources of the epic poet, the literary critic,
the Augustian satirist, the biographer, the historian, the
author of Childe Harold, the storytellers in taverns and
in Renaissance narratives, and a great many more, he contemplates the composition and evolution of styles, the

interplay of styles of living and writing with their respective traditions and with each other and, especially, the types of demands they make for attention within the competitive structure of his poem.

But, lest this sound too serious, and not at all like the poem we remember, Don Juan is, with one possible exception, an appreciation of limitations and failures of style, propelled by a kind of comic repulsion toward any available human voice. That is to say, among other things, that Byron--except, perhaps, for Juan's decision to rescue Leila in Canto VIII, choosing, as he does in the language of Jack Johnson's command, between "your fame and feelings, pride and pity"--never makes any special claims about the superiority of a style or a set of styles. The poem is particularly adept in elaborating the various ways in which a style may fail, in describing the inability of a style to control the problems it, presumably, has been invented to solve. The forms and qualities of failure in Don Juan are especially diverse and impressive because Byron almost never belies the complexities of his subjects. Styles fail in this poem for more 'reasons' and combinations of 'reasons' than is necessary to specify here. A style, for instance, might no longer be supported by its traditions, those traditions may have become decadent, or in some other fashion outmoded and devitalized; the style may be required to consider situations outside of and inconsistent with its traditions. A style may be an extreme or exaggerated version of an otherwise lively tradtion with the result that the style becomes simple minded, or grotesque or ends up denying itself or the complexities implanted in the tradition. Or failure may be apprehended as the necessary consequence of having a style, any style. Each of the features of Don Juan I wish to discuss here participates in these and related failures of style; but they also concern themselves, more specifically, with the passage of a style through time. The styles the poem considers most often are ones caught up in or leaning towards detritus. Byron focuses upon the temporal processes which render a style--both thoroughly developed and articulated ones such as romance, or pastoral, or epic, and those which, ostensibly, are more immediate and spontaneous--obsolete, and mark it moribund and as waste. He summons and examines the languages that compose a style, pursuing them as the feats of association and imaginative prowess they originally structured and sustained pass into vapidity, into cliche, or the word that he uses most often to describe this, into cant. I would like to look at some of the forms of cant Byron reproduces or invents in Don Juan.

    The first appearance of the word occurs in the opening stanza of the poem as Byron separates Don Juan from a number of contemporary political and military heroes:

> "I want a hero, an uncommon want
>   When every year and month sends forth a new one,
> Till after cloying the gazettes with cant,
>   The age discovers he is not the true one.
> Of such as these I should not care to vaunt;
>   I'll therefore take our ancient friend Don Juan."
>   (I.1)[1]

"Cloying" is an especially appropriate gerund to link with

"cant," combining, as it does, notions of cheating and deception with those of obstruction, clogging, and an overindulgence that passes beyond desire ("want") into loathing and weariness. This attitude is consistent with virtually all of the subsequent direct references to "cant" in the poem. For example, in the fourth canto Byron writes,

> "I once had great alacrity in wielding
> My pen and like poetic war to wage
> And recollect the time when all this cant
> Would have provoked remarks, which now it shan't."
>
> (IV.98)

The allusion is to the reception of the poem's initial cantos, to the probability expressed earlier as "Through needle's eyes it easier for the camel is/To pass than those two cantos into families." A similar conception of cant lies behind a number of stanzas in which the word does not appear; many of these occur in the London cantos, or in the cantos describing the Russian assault upon Ismail. Byron dedicates Cantos IX-XI to Napoleon in this manner:

> "As these new cantos touch on warlike feats,
> To you the unflattering Muse deigns to inscribe
> Truths that you will not read in the gazettes,
> But which ('tis time to teach the hireling tribe
> Who fatten on their country's gore and debts)
> Must be recited, and without a bribe.
> You did great things, but not being great in mind
> Have left undone the greatest--and mankind."
>
> (IX.10)

In each of these passages Byron clearly presents his narrator as a moral and literary iconoclast, penetrating sham and hypocrisy and reputation to reveal priggishness, sentimentality, deceit, arrogance, insensitivity, stupidity, and abuses of language and trust. This same narrative posture

informs many of Byron's specific attacks and parodies--
those of Wordsworth (I.90-91; III.93-100; IV.109; VIII.9),
Southey (I.222; III.97), Malthus (I.131; XI.30; XII.14, 20;
XV.37-38), Berkeley (XI.1-6), Petrarch (I.87-89), and so on--
where he deflates a well-known style or attitude through
careful appropriations of diction and tone or, more tellingly (in a fashion familiar to Pope in The Art of Sinking in Poetry and the second Dunciad, and to many practitioners of Pop Art), by direct quotation.

Presumably, it is these stanzas, and others similar to them, that have prompted almost everyone who has written about the poem to produce a version of "a searingly honest man, impatient with cant from whatever source it came."[2] Yet, while it is possible to cite more passages of this type (consider, for example, VII.86; XII.40; or, IX.1) there are remarkably few instances in Don Juan where Byron chooses to dramatize literary iconoclasm so straightforwardly, or where his narrators are so secure and so uncomplicated about the methods and motives of their idol-smashing. Like so many aspects of the poem, this can be deceptive; the invocation in Canto VIII appears to be right in line with the stanzas I just quoted or referred to:

>   "Oh blood and thunder! And oh blood and wounds!
>   These are but vulgar oaths as you may deem,
>   Too gentle reader, and most shocking sounds.
>   And so they are; yet this is glory's dream
>   Unriddled, and as my true Muse expounds
>   At present such things, since they are her theme,
>   So be they her inspirers. Call them Mars,
>   Bellona, what you will--they mean but wars."
>   (VIII.1)

Ruthlessly, Byron's "true Muse" rewrites the opening lines of the preceding canto: "Oh Love! Oh Glory," deftly, becomes "Oh Blood and Thunder," exposing the vulgarities of war to an audience it regards as unaccustomed to the truth. If what he is introducing, again in an echo of Canto VII, is "glory's dream unriddled" he is also unriddling the heroic language which classical and contemporary writers of epic, and of martial literature, generally bring to descriptions of battle, and which this audience ("what you will") has been educated to expect. Against this he opposes his own poetic "shocking sounds." He, first, satirically arrogates some key terms of that language ("Muse," "theme," "inspirers"), and then demolishes them: "Call them Mars,/Bellona,...--they mean but wars."

The style of the succeeding stanza follows from this literary purgation:

> "All was prepared--the fire, the sword, the men
>   To wield them in their terrible array."

The poem strikes a tone not inconsistent with presentations in works of history, or even in journalism; each of the major nouns is more or less subject to ostensive definition, and a far cry from the personifications of epic. But immediately and typically the language changes. The progress of the Russian army is compared first to the stalking of "a lion from its den" and then to

> "A human Hydra...issuing from its fen
>   To breathe destruction on its winding way,
>   Whose heads were heroes, which cut off in vain,
>   Immediately in others grew again."

Drawing upon Homer and Vergil, reproducing their conceited

diction as well as some stylizations from portraiture, Byron--in a manner not at all dissimilar to Norman Mailer's appropriation of reportorial conventions in *Armies of the Night*--has slipped into a poetic style he has just elucidated and denounced. That he did not pause to excise the passage does not really follow from the method he describes in Canto IX as "I cannot stop to alter words once written," as Helen Gardner's corrective essay on the manuscripts of *Don Juan* has established.[3] Byron is calling attention, first of all, to the fact that the events recorded in these lines are no more significant or 'real' than the stylistic resources he can bring to them, or the act and experience of writing them. But, more immediately, he is contesting the hierarchy he has just invented and questioning the exclusivity of what might be called the voice of realism ("my true Muse"), and its claim to superiority over representations in epics. The stanza that follows comments upon this:

>   "History can only take things in the gross;
>   But could we know them in detail, perchance...
>   The drying up a single tear has more
>   Of honest fame than shedding seas of gore."
>   (VIII.3)

Byron considers the ways in which each of these styles of writing history inevitably distorts, projecting, as they do, "Mars," "Bellona," lions, Hydras, as well as conceptions as indefinite and vague as "men," sword," "army" and "array." His demonstration points to the availability of iconoclasm to the writer of realism in much the same way that other forms of sincerity are available to the writer of, say, pastoral.

Byron's awareness of just how highly charged and conditioned are the languages reproduced in works of literature prevents him from projecting the stable linguistic and hence, dramatic, center that uncomplicated iconoclasm presupposes. But while this recognition can be subsumed within a larger and more general argument about the boundaries of language, more often, it seems to be prompted by tremendous suspicions about the stability and coherency commonly assumed to be present in the forms of ordinary life. Byron almost never seeks support and confirmation for a style, or a tone, or a statement in these forms--whether these are historical, journalistic, scientific, legal, poetic or personal. Rather he approaches each of these as kinds or types of discourse subject to the same distortive conditioning and fictionalizing processes as those that exist in literature, and demanding the same type of close attention if their shaping figures and metaphors are not to degenerate into cant. <u>Don Juan</u> is filled with comic appreciations of the ways in which an event comes to be regarded as true. For example, early in Canto I, Byron proffers his narrator in the guise of a judicious biographer giving the lie to the rumor that Juan's mother had slept with Don Alfonso before his marriage to Julia:

> "Julia was--yet I never could see why--
>   With Donna Inez quite a favourite friend;
> Between their tastes there was small sympathy,
>   For not a line had Julia ever penned.
> Some people whisper (but no doubt they lie,
>   For malice still imputes some private end)
> That Inez had, ere Don Alfonso's marriage,
> Forgot with him her very prudent carriage."
>   (I.66)

In the stanza that follows, however, the narrator's posture returns to that of the sly, gossipy Spanish storyteller ("a cigar in his mouth, a jug of Malaga or perhaps 'right sherris' before him on a small table") Byron proposed in the "Preface to Cantos I and II":

> "And that still keeping up the odd connexion,
>   Which time had lately rendered much more chaste,
> She took his lady also in affection.
>   And certainly this course was much the best."
>   (I.67)

The cynicism, the effort to deflate moral and social superiority and, above all, the conviction present in his last comment push the "lie" well on the road to fact. Finally, by the end of the canto--"Julia in fact had tolerable ground;/Alfonso's loves with Inez were well known" (I.176)-- Donna Inez's indiscretions have become common property and take their place in a tradition that is, apparently, inviolable and unquestionable.

Byron is even more suspicious about any claims to accuracy and certainty that have been or might be made in the name of history. Throughout *Don Juan* he refuses to consider history except as a form of literary discourse, except as a collection of history books. Very early in the poem he alludes to Horace's ode in praise of Lullius (*Ode* IV.9) citing these lines, "<u>Vixere ortes ante</u> Agamemnona/ <u>multi; sed omnes inlacrimabiles/urgentur ignotique longa/ nocte, carent quia vate sacra</u>." Repeatedly, he translates, paraphrases or echoes this passage in order to emphasize the shaping presence of the historian and biographer in what comes to be apprehended as factual or true. In Canto III he explicitly approaches history as imaginative literature:

> "And glory long has made the sages smile;
>   'Tis something, nothing, words, illusion, wind,
> Depending more upon the historian's style
>   Than on the name a person leaves behind.
> Troy owes to Homer what whist owes to Hoyle.
>   The present century was growing blind
> To the great Marlborough's skill in giving knocks
> Until his late <u>Life</u> by Archdeacon Coxe."
> (III.90)

Later in the poem he turns from isolated and individual acts of historicizing to successive and collective ones:

> "Of poets who come down to us through distance
>   Of time and tongues, the foster babes of Fame,
> Life seems the smallest portion of existence.
>   Where twenty ages gather o'er a name,
> 'Tis as a snowball which derives assistance
>   From every flake and yet rolls on the same,
> Even till an iceberg it may chance to grow,
> But after all 'tis nothing but cold snow."
> (IV.100)

Or, again, in one of his frequent puns, he writes, "And so great names are nothing more than nominal." But the most thorough denunciation of <u>a priori</u> standards of verification, and of rigid distinctions between literary shapings and, ostensibly, non-fictional ones occurs when Byron begins to separate his poem from classical epics, arguing that "this story's actually true." He justifies his remark in this manner:

> "If any person doubt it, I appeal
>   To history, tradition, and to facts,
> To newspapers, whose truth all know and feel
>   To plays in five, and operas in three acts.
> All these confirm my statement a good deal,
>   But that which more completely faith exacts
> Is that myself and several now in Seville
> Saw Juan's last elopement with the devil."
> (I.203)

Here he refuses to distinguish among journalistic accounts, history, fiction, folklore, gossip, presentations in plays and in operas, autobiography and personal recollections. Each of the enterprises which compose his "appeal" are constructs of the imagination and, as such, must be available for criticism to the imagination that has allowed them to make sense. Byron equalizes the demands that each of these make, both as codifications of significance and of source materials outside of the poem, and for his--and our--consideration of it. None has a unique, or even special, status.

Prominent in this attempt to demystify and equalize the claims made in the service of 'reality' or 'truth' is the recognition that no articulated style can be thought of as innocent, can be apprehended as independent of, or unvitiated by, the forces of human contrivance. In Don Juan, Byron obviously considers the languages of history, or of journalism, or of autobiography to be as historicized and as conditioned as those which compose what is more immediately and widely recognized as imaginative literature. Moreover, in almost every stage, the poem is informed by an awareness of the awesome degree to which ordinary life is composed, conventionalized, and stereotyped previous to any authorial or, simply, individual presence.[4] As he writes, in one of the stanzas I referred to earlier, "Life seems the smallest portion of existence." Central to the metaphor which follows--a ball of snow rolling down a mountain--is an acknowledgement of the special authority that resides in mankind's collective constructions. Byron appreciates the power of myths, systems, traditions, accumu-

lations of meaning, styles and historical resonances--
often proceeding from no identifiable, individual source--
to choke isolated expressive acts. In Canto XV, speaking
of the difficulties involved in delineating character,
he writes, "The difference is that in days of old,/Men made
the manners; manners now make men." He also understands
how an unreflective adoption of the props, assumptions, and
language of these enterprises is another form of cant,
and can lead to the repression of the intellectual, emotional and imaginative energies they originally sustained,
structured and set free.

Byron's uncertainties as to what tradition, myth or
formal pose may be speaking behind and through any, ostensibly, personal acts of expression lead him to deflate,
or more actively, denounce--in the very process of setting
them down-the voices and styles he presents in Don Juan.
The poem proceeds by strategies and movements of disloca-
tion, distancing and self-parody. Rather often these are
explicit, as when he directly disowns a figure or a statement: "But this simile is trite and stupid" (I.55); or
"an Arab Horse, a stately stag, a barb/New broke, came-
leopard, a gazelle--/No, none of these will do" (II.6);
or "As a volcano holds the lava more/Within, et cetera.
Shall I go on? No./I hate to hunt down a tired metaphor
(XIII.36). Paralleling this are his parodic attempts to
evaluate, to explain or otherwise to read a metaphor he has
just summoned: "That's an appropriate simile" (IX.27); or
"This metaphor, I think, holds good as aught" (VII.49). At

one point he concludes a collection of comparisons with
"...or like--like nothing that I know/except itself"
(XVI.10). Elsewhere he announces that a simile he has just
employed is a cliche:

> "'Twas midnight, Donna Julia was in bed,
>   Sleeping, most probably, when at her door
> Arose a clatter might awake the dead,
>   If they had never been awake before,
> And that they have been so we all have read,
>   And are to be so, at the least, once more."
>   (I.136)

Occasionally, he anticipates a reader's possible reaction
and acts it out: "Ah, well--a--day,/My teeth begin to chatter, my veins freeze" (I.181); or he invites the reader to
shift gears and do a bit of writing for him: "...--or
what you will./My similes are gathered in a heap,/So pick
and choose" (VI.68); or he blurs distinction between the
readers he inserts into the text (see, for example, II.13),
and those who might actually be looking at a copy of it:

> "I feel this tediousness will never do;
>   'Tis being too epic, and I must cut it down
> (In copying) this long canto into two.
>   They'll never find it out, unless I own
> The fact, excepting some experienced few
>   And then as an improvement 'twill be shown."
>   (III.111)

He also fills his poem with extended reading or grammar
'lessons,' as in Canto I (122-127) when he reproduces the
word "sweet" in a variety of contexts, at once defining it
and exposing its limitations as a descriptive term for
poetry, or later in the same canto when he discusses why
his poem is, or is not, "epic." In manner and intention
Byron's 'lessons' compare, for instance, with Shakespeare's
in A Midsummer Night's Dream (where he focuses on words like

"fair," "right," "reason," "love," "dreams," "comedy," "tragedy") or Pope's in "An Essay on Criticism" ("wit," "nature," "critic," etc.).

A more common way in which Byron immediately disowns a style he has just employed is the introduction of a stanza, usually comic but not necessarily or always (as often he upsets his comic styles, as well), into the poem that so obviously, in tone or content, clashes with those around it, that it has the effect of, at least, calling them into question, if not actually and thoroughly destroying them. The essence of this procedure, of course, consists in the narrator's timing; and more often than not, Byron drops these stanzas at precisely the point when they can do the greatest damage. There are far too many stanzas of this type in <u>Don Juan</u> to discuss or even to list here. And their basic character and function in the poem is so obvious as well, that I shall limit myself to only a few of the more paradigmatic and successful ones. For instance, one feature of the poem that is often isolated for description and praise is that which, in the curious words of Elizabeth French Boyd, "epitomizes the prosaic, tough realism with which he elected to relate a scene hallowed by romance"[5]--that is, Byron's treatment of the wreck of the "Trinidada" in Canto II. Other critics have gone so far as to connect this episode, and the cantos on the Russian-Turkish War with what they term the realistic novel of the eighteenth and nineteenth centuries.[6] Yet, what is generally forgotten or overlooked is that the poem's progress toward "realism" is continually disrupted by stanzas of this sort:

> "All the rest perished; near two hundred souls
>   Had left their bodies. And what's worse, alas,
> When over Catholics the ocean rolls,
>   They must wait several weeks before a mass
> Takes off one peck of purgatorial coals,
>   Because, till people know what's come to pass,
> They won't lay out their money on the dead.
> It costs three francs for every mass that's said.
>   (II.55)
>
> Up came John Johnson (I will not say Jack,
>   For that were vulgar, cold, and commonplace
> On great occasions, such as an attack
>   On cities, as hath been the present case)--
> Up Johnson came with hundreds at his back,
>   Exclaiming 'Juan, Juan.' On, boy, brace
> Your arm, and I'll bet Moscow to a dollar
> That you and I will win St. George's collar."
>   (VIII.97)

The sentence set off in brackets here suggests just how sophisticated Byron is in regard to the styles he adopts; in a comically pedantic effort to preserve the high, almost heroic, tone he has sustained for half-a-dozen stanzas, he wrecks it.

Very often, he uses his disruptive stanzas as a restraint upon rhetorical pompousness, or pretentiousness. He inserts them when a narrator approaches didacticism or, in some other manner, begins to take his role or his presentation too seriously. One of the most effective instances of this occurs in Canto IX:

> "Oh ye great authors luminous, voluminous!
>   Ye twice ten hundred thousand daily scribes
> Whose pamphlets, volumes, newspapers illumine us!
>   Whether you're paid by government in bribes
> To prove the public debt is not consuming us.
>   Or roughly treading on the 'courtier's kibes'
> With clownish heel, your popular circulation
> Feeds you by printing half the realm's starvation--
>
> Oh ye great authors! <u>Apropos</u> <u>des</u> <u>bottes</u>
>   I have forgotten what I meant to say,

>   As sometimes have been great sages' lots.
>   'Twas something calculated to allay
>   All wrath in barracks, palaces, or cots.
>   Certes it would have been but thrown away,
>   And that's one comfort for my lost advice,
>   Although no doubt it was beyond all price."
>   (IX.35-36)

The poem frequently exploits a narrator's forgetfulness, ignorance, or confusion in its attempt to deflate and disown voices and styles. Byron's travesty of the narrative convention that entered scientific thought with Galileo, Albertie, and, most importantly, Descartes, and which was quickly taken up by Richardson and Defoe--a solitary witness imposing a kind of frame upon an experience--is, generally, no less devastating or comic than Sterne's or Diderot's or Beckett's.[7]

Consistent with these efforts to contaminate any high or deeply serious tone is the poem's appropriation of classical and Renaissance literature. Virtually all of the allusions to Greek, Roman, and Italian culture in <u>Don Juan</u> are, in some way, ironic: either they are inaccurate, inappropriate, or misapplied. In one of his most brilliant comments upon his own work, Byron refers to this as "sinking the allegory." He writes

>   "I say that beef is rare, and can't help thinking
>   That the old fable of Minotaur--
>   From which our modern morals, rightly shrinking,
>   Condemn the royal lady's taste who wore
>   A cow's shape for a mask--was only (sinking
>   The allegory) a mere type; no more,
>   The Pasiphae promoted breeding cattle,
>   To make the Cretans bloodier in battle."
>   (II.155)

The passage provides, perhaps, the most interesting illustration of the phrase. Byron sets aside traditional interpretations of the episode that point to betrayal, retribution, ingratitude, the nature of love, the power of darkness, and the political dominance of Crete over Athens in favor of an argument that asserts--only--the protein-value of beefsteak. Or in Canto I he paraphrases Horace (<u>Ode</u> IV, i) as he asserts that he has abandoned love that than no more will the "heart...be my sole world, my universe":

> "My days of love are over, me no more
>   The charms of maid, wife, and still less of widow
> Can make the fool of which they made before;
>   In short, I must not lead the life I did do.
> The credulous hope of mutual minds is o'er..."
> (I.216)

The narrator carefully forgets that in <u>his</u> poem Horace is declaring that he is in love again; also, he is announcing his return to lyric poetry. As this is done in the context of a set of poems and a tradition that specifically denounce epic poetry (see, especially, <u>Ode</u> III.iii), it is an unusual citation from a poet who, only seven stanzas earlier, referred to his "epical pretensions to the laurel." Or, again, Byron transforms one of the most powerful and moving passages in the <u>Inferno</u> into a justification of the presentation of cannibalism in literature:

> "And if Pedrillo's fate should shocking be,
>   Remember Ugolino condescends
> To eat the head of his archenemy,
>   The moment after he politely ends
> His tale. If foes be food in hell, at sea
>   'tis surely fair to dine upon friends
> When shipwreck's short allowance grows too scanty,
> Without being much more horrible than Dante."
> (II.83)

He also incorrectly records or ascribes a number of quotations in an effort to undercut their value and cogency. For instance, he alters (as he explains, in the interest of "the English rhyme") the phrase <u>medio tutissimus ibis</u>, and attributes it to Horace rather than to Ovid (VI.17). Some more general examples of "sinking the allegory" occur when he discusses, as he often does, the usefulness of published poetry as a lining material for portmanteau, or when he describes the liberalizing qualities of the grand tour as "and what's travel,/Unless it teaches one to quote and cavil?"

In <u>Don Juan</u>, Byron as self-parodist pays scrupulous attention to the passage of time, particularly to the way that time defiles the orders and figures posed by any speaking voice. One prominent example of this can be discerned if we focus upon the progress of Julia's letter to Juan through the poem. In six stanzas (I.192-197) she sets down her love for Juan, the fact that this love has completely destroyed her as a woman and as a human being ("for that love have lost/State, station, heaven, mankind's, my own esteem...Man's love is of his life a thing apart,/'Tis woman's whole existence."), and despite all this, that she has no regrets about the affair ("And yet cannot regret what it hath cost,/So dear is the memory of that dream."). She then proceeds to a convent and Juan is sent on a therapeutic tour of France and Italy. The next time her letter appears in the poem is when Juan is at sea; he rereads it, and addresses her in this manner:

> "'And oh, if e'er I should forget, I swear--
> But that's impossible and cannot be.
> Sooner shall this blue ocean melt to air,

>   Sooner shall earth resolve itself to sea
> Than I resign thine image, oh my fair!
>   Or think on anything excepting thee.
> A mind diseased no remedy can physic.'
> (Here the ship gave a lurch, and he grew seasick.)
>
> 'Sooner shall heaven kiss earth' (here he fell
>   sicker)--
>   'Oh Julia, what is every other woe?'
> (For God's sake let me have a glass of liquor,
>   Pedro, Battista, help me down below.)
> 'Julia, my love (you rascal, Pedro, quicker),
>   Oh Julia (this curst vessel pitches so),
> Beloved Julia, hear me still beseeching!'
> (Here he grew inarticulate with retching.)
>
> He felt that chilling heaviness of heart,
>   Or rather stomach, which alas, attends,
> Beyond the best apothecary's art,
>   The loss of love, the treachery of friends,
>   Or the death of those we dote on, when a part
> Of us dies with them as each fond hope ends.
> No doubt he would have been much more pathetic,
> But the sea acted as a strong emetic."
>   (II.19-21)

These stanzas are among the most vicious of the poem. With a cleverness that is almost flagitious, Byron tramples upon the emotions that Juan is attempting to express, as well as those contained in Julia's letter. Skillfully he literalizes the tropes and traditions of romantic and heroic love that secure an analogue for emotional disturbances ("A mind diseased," "that chilling heaviness of heart," "when a part/ Of us dies") in physical sickness; in doing so, he renders them contemptible and absurd. The metaphors that Juan relies upon to describe the durability of his love are, in another sense, literalized, as without exception they are drawn from the storm that surrounds him and that, comically, competes with Julia for his attention. The passage also plays with the notion that strong emotions are somehow inconsistent with, and beyond, language: "'Beloved Julia, hear me still beseeching!'/(Here he grew inarticulate with retching.)" But the most important feature of these stanzas consists in Byron's flawless sense of pacing and dramatic timing, achieved primarily by unobtrusive parallelisms ("Sooner... than," "Here"), a witty use of parentheses, and the learned, jocular commentary that quietly concludes Juan's strained, wracked, soliloquy.

The third appearance of the note is almost anticlimactic. The "Trinidada" has finally been wrecked by the storm; thirty or so passengers repair to a life boat. But, lacking food, they begin to speak "of lots for flesh and blood,/ And who should die to be his fellow's food..."

> "And then they looked around them and despaired,
>   And none to be the sacrifice would choose.
> At length the lots were torn up and prepared,
>   But of materials that much shock the Muse.
> Having no paper, for the want of better,
> They took by force from Juan Julia's letter."
> (II.73-74)

Again, Byron emphasizes the physical. The destruction of the piece of paper emblematically completes the destruction of the emotions it carried and provoked. Again, the scene involves sickness: "The consequence was awful in the extreme,/For they who were most ravenous in the act/Went raging mad. Lord! how they did blaspheme/And foam and roll with strong convulsions racked..."

Another more subtle and complicated instance of Byron's anxious attention to the passage of time is the Juan and Haidee episode, particularly his account of their love-making on the shore. He sets them walking along the beach in two of the poem's most sympathetic and endearing stanzas:

> "And thus they wandered forth, and hand in hand,
>   Over the shining pebbles and the shells,
> Glided along the smooth and hardened sand,
>   And in the worn and wild receptacles
> Worked by the storms, yet worked as it were planned.
>   In hollow halls with sparry roofs and cells,
> They turned to rest, and each clasped by an arm,
> Yielded to the deep twilight's purple charm.
>
> They looked up to the sky, whose floating glow
>   Spread like a rosy ocean, vast and bright.
> They gazed upon the glittering sea below,
>   Whence the broad moon rose circling into sight.
> They heard the wave's splash and the wind so low,
>   And saw each other's dark eyes darting light
> Into each other, and beholding this,
> Their lips drew near and clung into a kiss."
>   (II.184-185)

The narrator seems to be completely caught up in the events he is recording as nature (nature approached as an agent of art, "yet worked as it were planned") and time conspire to shape a scene of almost classical beauty. But immediately he begins to detach and distance himself from the situation by bringing to it a sophistication that it cannot bear. Like Wordsworth taking "the knife in hand/And stopping not at parts less sensitive," he probes and examines their kiss. He writes that "a kiss's strength/I think...must be reckoned by its length" and, pedantically concludes "By length I mean duration" (186-187). Byron then inserts into his description an historical and literary perspective--a tradition of foiled and wrecked loves--that Haidee is "ignorant" or "innocent" of; for her, "What was said or done/Elsewhere was nothing" (202). As he elaborates,

> "Haidee spoke not of scruples, asked no vows
>   Nor offered any; she had never heard
> Of plight and promises to be a spouse,
>   Or perils by a loving maid incurred.
> She was all which pure ignorance allows

> And flew to her young mate like a young bird.
> And never having dreamt of falsehood, she
> Had not one word to say of constancy."
> (II.190)

Later, he echoes Julia's letter to Juan and considers the dangers of loving specifically from a woman's viewpoint: "Alas, the love of women!...For all of theirs upon that die is thrown,/And if 'tis lost, life hath no more to bring/ To them but mockeries of the past alone...for man, to man so oft unjust,/Is always so to women" (199-200).

The narrator's rendition of their love-making is also informed by his own temporal and historical perspective, which, elsewhere, he describes as "the sad truth which hovers o'er my desk/Turns what was once romantic to burlesque" (IV.3). He introduces this section of Canto ll by announcing that he is through with "women and friends." They are "but dreams of what has been, no more to be...As for the ladies...I, like other 'dogs, have had my day'" (166). This attitude determines many of the specific terms and postures of his language. Condescendingly, he classifies their kisses as those which "belong to early days" (186). Gazing upon them in the final moments of passion, he sighs "And oh, that quickening of the heart, that beat!/How much it costs us!" (203). He addresses love in a fashion that recalls his early poem "To Romance": "Oh Love, thou art the very god of evil,/For after all we cannot call thee devil" (205). Occasionally he approaches his young lovers as if they are a pair of domesticated animals. Haidee reaches out to "her young mate like a young bird" (190); daily, she goes to the cave "to see her bird reposing in his nest./And she would softly stir his locks so curly..." (168). In these lines the poem stops just short of referring to Juan as her pet: "It was such a pleasure to behold him, such enlargement of existence to partake/Nature with him...To watch him slumbering and to see him wake...He was her own, her ocean treasure, cast/Like a rich wreck, her first love and her last" (173). His most brutal comment upon their love occurs in the proem to Canto III where, with Juan still asleep on the sand and Haidee lying beside him, he describes her as "too deeply blest/To feel the poison through her spirit creeping." The narrator's disgust has passed from the metaphors and the traditions and the sentimentality that surround sexual love to the biological act itself.

Byron removes himself most completely from the scene he is setting down at precisely that moment when Juan and Haidee are most involved with one another. He writes:

>"They look upon each other, and their eyes
>   Gleam in the moonlight, and her white arm clasps
>Round Juan's head, and his around hers lies
>   Half buried in the tresses which it grasps.
>She sits upon his knee and drinks his sighs,
>   He hers, until they end in broken gasps;
>And thus they form a group that's quite antique
>Half naked, loving, natural, and Greek."
>   (II.194)

In his final couplet, Byron transforms the tremendous emotional and physical energies of the preceeding lines into a stasis that approaches mere prettiness, and presents the lovers as if they were a work of art, specifically, a piece of sculpture. There is in Don Juan what might be termed a pattern of aestheticizing very strong or very painful emotions. For instance, Pedrillo's remains are said to have "regaled" two sharks, as though Juan's tutor were performing in an aquatic theater of cruelty (II.77); or, when Leila is in her moment of greatest pain and danger her face is described as "like to a lighted alabaster vase" (VIII.96). In a more obvious example of this, the narrator's only immediate response to Julia's letter is an appreciation of the stock on which it is written:

> "This note was written upon gilt-edged paper
>   With a neat crow quill, rather hard but new.
> Her small white fingers scarce could reach the
>   taper,
>   But trembles as magnetic needles do,
> And yet she did not let one tear escape her.
>   The seal a sunflower; <u>Elle vous suit partout</u>,
> The motto, cut upon a white cornelian;
> The wax was superfine, its hue vermillion."
>   (I.198)

Moreover, some of the cogency of the letter itself was removed when Byron decided to locate the affair within the conventional temporal frame of classical and medieval romances: "It was upon a day, a summer's day--/Summer's indeed a very dangerous season,/And so is spring about the end of May" (I. 102). And finally, his first description of Juan as he lies wrecked on the shore very closely parallels his later one of the lovers: "And like a withered lily, on the land/His slender frame and pallid aspect lay,/As fair a thing as e'er was formed of clay." His punning upon "clay"-- a synonym for flesh and a material for statues--in that it emphasizes the role of artifice in the situation, also draws attention to the conventionality of the phrase "like a withered lily," a judgment he reinforces through repetition (see, for example, the comparison of Juan to "a young flower snapped from the stalk" in II.176).

In each of these passages, Byron's narrator encounters his subjects with the assumptions, interests, and values of a performer-critic. He readjusts his conceptual frames, shifting his attention from the individual demands of these subjects in a search for alternative ways in which they might be imagined or understood. His solution is that of an aesthete. He makes sense of, and redeems, pain, violence, death, and uncontrolled, intense emotion by immediately giving form to them, by aestheticizing them; he provides contexts in which they may be approached as works of art, and furthermore, beautiful and comic works of art. In the process he also transforms his relationship with Juan, Haidee, Julia, Leila and Pedrillo: he withdraws and distances himself to the point where direct involvement is no longer necessary or possible. All that was bothersome, ugly, and painful about them disappears beneath his "affectless gaze."[8] As such, his attitude can also be described as voyeuristic; this voyeurism, however is not sexual but almost exclusively aesthetic, or is sexual only to the extent that sex is an aspect of human behavior. He absents himself from a potentially painful and disturbing dramatic situation, exchanging the gestures and tones of personal involvement for a quality that might best be labelled presence. The new contexts he provides and the quality of presence reside in the way he chooses to look at his subjects, that is, in the act of gazing itself. Consciousness then becomes a theater, becomes an art gallery.

As I attempted to demonstrate above, <u>Don Juan</u> is a work exclusively composed of what might best be termed "contexts."[9] Byron, here, treats all of his voices as equals. Reading the poem we sense that no voice is making a stronger claim for our attention than any other, that there is no voice that is more than provisionally or contextually interesting and compelling. As Paul West has written of Byron, "Reduce everything he ever wrote, and you will find an essential act of repulsion: either self-emptying into a <u>persona</u>, or a repudiation. He pushes away what he is...He shows himself only to be pointless or to vitiate."[10] Byron provides his own best commentary upon his writing in the opening stanzas of Canto IV.

> "If from great Nature's or our own abyss
>   Of thought we could but snatch a certainty,
> Perhaps mankind might find the path they miss,
>   But then 'twould spoil much good philosophy,
> One system eats another up, and this
>   Much as old Saturn ate his progeny
> For when his pious consort gave him stones
> In lieu of sons, of these he made no bones.
>
> But System doth reverse the Titan's breakfast
>   And eats her parents, albeit the digestion
> Is difficult. Pray, tell me, can you make fast
>   After due search your faith to any question?
> Look back o'er ages ere unto the stake fast
>   You bind yourself and call some mode the best
>   one.
> Nothing more true than not to trust your senses,
> And yet what are your other evidences?
>
> For me, I know nought. Nothing I deny,
>   Admit, reject, contemn; and what know <u>you</u>
> Except perhaps that you were born to die?"
>   (XIV.1-3)

The sentence which begins "One system eats another up..." circumscribes both the epistemological premises and assumptions that propel the poem forward, and the literary devices that compose it. Perhaps what is most essential about <u>Don Juan</u> is the fact that it is unfinished--not just literally so, but that at every stage Byron refuses to conclude, refuses to accommodate his styles and voices within an hierarchy, and refuses to allow any shaping presence, including his own, to belie the difficulties inherent in any attempt to think or to act or to write. When he writes phrases like "I sketch your world exactly as it goes" or "this story's actually true" or "my Muse by no means deals in fiction," occasionally he is simply annotating one of the poses available to the writer of realism in a manner I described earlier. But more often he is suggesting that he is giving free play--in so far as this is possible in a formal work that is subject to the demands of rhythm and rhyme--to the literary, social and political languages he hears around him. It is possible to say, I think, that the poem has no character of its own. Here, in contrast with his procedure in most of his other long poems, Byron never elaborates a personal style that he might apply on any occasion. The style--in the broadest sense of the word--like the characters of each of its different narrators, is receptive rather than imposing. A central paradox of the poem is that while it can be argued that in <u>Don Juan</u> Byron secured his most successful vehicle for self-dramatization, this dramatization takes the form of a self-effacing invisibility. The notion that an autobiography which is scrupulously self-measuring and attentive to its immediate modes of rendition may compose an elaborate disappearing act was present in <u>Childe</u>

<u>Harold</u> in so far as both the Childe and his narrators are so demonstrably <u>personae</u>. The terms of this self-effacement are suggested more specifically in Canto III of that poem where he writes "Tis to create, and in creating live/A being more intense that we endow/With form and fancy, gaining as we give/The life we image, even as I do now--/What am I? Nothing: but not so art thou,/Soul of my thought!" (III.6). Later in the same canto he announces

>"I live not in myself, but I become
> Portion of that around me..."
>   (III.86)

But in <u>Don Juan</u> Byron is more sophisticated and playful about his acts of self-effacement. When he boasts "For I have more than one Muse at a push" (X.5) he is, in the language of Keats's famous letter to Richard Woodhouse, "everything and nothing." His sounds from stanza to stanza are those of the events he records and (in another sense) invents. As he writes,

>"For checkered as is seen our human lot
>   With good and bad and worse, alike prolific
> Of melancholy merriment; to quote
>   Too much of one sort would be soporific
> Without, or with, offense to friends or foes,
> I sketch your world exactly as it goes."
>   (VIII.89)

Finally, as the phrase "to quote/Too much of one sort would be soporific" suggests, what interests Byron about a style is the uses that might be made of it in the poem he is writing, the occasions it may provide for his own performances. He indicates that it is only <u>Don Juan</u> that matters in a number of ways. He carefully confuses his realms, blurring distinctions between the realities that literature and art propose and those directed by other kinds of imaginative acts. For example, in this passage he fuses liberty of subject matter with liberty of style, proceeding as if he were about to describe a sexual act graphically (the context is Julia's seduction of Juan) only to redefine "chastity" as an element of Aristotelian decorum:

> "Here my chaste Muse a liberty must take
> Start not, still chaster reader, she'll be nice
> hence--
> Forward, and there is no great cause to quake.
> This liberty is a poetic license,
> Which some irregularity may make
> In the design, and as I have a high sense
> Of Aristotle and the rules, 'tis fit
> To beg his pardon when I err a bit.
>
> The license is to hope the reader will
> Suppose...that several months have passed."
> (I.120-121)

This attitude influences his descriptions of his characters, particularly of Don Juan. Playfully, he writes "Don Juan, who was real or ideal--/For both are much the same" (X.20); and, more literally, he refers to Juan as "a child of song" (VIII.24). Frequently, he presents an event in terms of the physical properties of a published book, or by means of the formal divisions of his poem. When he decides to abandon a sad, gloomy tone he has struck for what he believes to be too many stanzas, he speaks of laying "this sheet of sorrows on the shelf" (IV.74); when Lambro secures a group of slaves in the hold of his ship he is said to have "Chained/His prisoners, dividing them like chapters/In numbered lots..." (III.15); when Juan is threatened, Byron first considers his poem, and then his hero's life: "Lambro presented, and one instant more/Had stopped this canto and Don Juan's breath" IV.42); or, when many of the Russian soldiers have been killed at Ismail he refers to their column as "now reduced, as is a bulky volume/Into an elegant extract (much less massy)/Of heroism..." (VIII.34).

There are many occasions in the poem when Byron pauses to announce that he has just altered or redirected an event in order to adjust it to his metrical and formal scheme. I mentioned earlier that he rewrites a passage from Horace for this reason (VI.17-18). This also determines which of Adeline's house guests appear in the poem: "I have named a few, not foremost in degree,/But ta'en at hazard as the rhyme may run" (XIII.83); or at one point, he introduces an archaism ("whilk") by saying, "The rhyme obliges me to do this; sometimes/Monarchs are less imperative than rhymes" (V.77); or, he justifies the appearance of a word he abhors ("tact") with the apology, "That modern phrase appears to me sad stuff,/But it will serve to keep my verse compact" (I.178); or, he translates a French cliche into a Latin one ("<u>inter nos</u>"), arguing "This should be <u>entre nous</u>, for Julia thought/In French, but then the rhyme would go for nought" (I.84). Rather often he plays upon the presumed connection between rhyme and sense: "Kiss rhymes to bliss in fact as well as verse" (VI.59); more directly and with greater wit he writes:

> "Besides Platonic love, besides the love
>   Of God, the love of sentiment, the loving
> Of faithful pairs (I needs must rhyme with dove
>   That good old steamboat which keeps verses moving
> 'Gainst reason. Reason ne'er was hand and glove
>   With rhyme, but always leant less to improving

> The sound than sense)--besides all these pretenses
> To love, there are those things..."
> (IX.74)

Each of these deliberated obfuscations and alterations is consistent with the critical remarks Byron drops in <u>Don Juan</u> about the role of statements, of efforts of understanding, and of moral considerations as opposed to that of the performing poet. Of any effort to censure literature on the ground of licentiousness he writes, "You may do right forbidding them to show 'em/But spoil (I think) a very pretty poem" (IV.107). And in a comic appropriation of the Vergilian <u>mirabile dictu</u> he describes Gulbeyaz' anger toward Juan in this fashion: "Nought's more sublime than energetic bile/Though horrible to see, yet grand to tell,/Like ocean warring 'gainst a rocky isle; And the deep passions flashing through her form/Made her a beautiful embodied storm" (V.135). In turn, virtually all of the metaphors Byron evolves for the writing of his poem involve some aspect of performance. In the <u>proem</u> to Canto VII he describes his poem as one "show" among many--"What after all are all things, but a show...And such as they are my present tale is" (VII.2). Or, again in the manner of Norman Mailer, he apprehends poetry in a language derived from athletic competition:

> "In twice five years the 'greatest living poet,'
> Like to the champion in the fisty ring,
> Is called on to support his claim or show it..."
> (XI.55)

As greater writers are akin to "champions" so poorer ones are regarded as "pretenders" (XI.61). Byron often approaches poetry as a performance, in the face of death, prompted by a desire for fame, love, applause, and the kind of secular redemption that fame and love often bestow. He asks, "had none admired,/Would Pope have sung or Horace been inspired?" (V.100); he identifies poets with Lucifer, "our sin the same...being pride..." (IV.1). Frequently, he considers his own popular success in a manner that has remarkably little to do with irony or cynicism:

> "Well, if I don't succeed, I have succeeded,
>   And that's enough; succeeded in my youth,
> The only time when much success is needed.
>   And my success produced what I in sooth
> Cared most about. It need not now be pleaded;
>   Whate'er it was, 'twas mine. I've paid, in truth
> Of late the penalty of such success,
> But have not learned to wish it any less."
>   (XII.17)

The phrase "what I in sooth/Cared most about" is pleonastic for fame; moreover, it is the conception of a fame that is, at once, immediate and pursued as an end in itself. The stanza occurs in the context of an argument as to which is the more valuable and necessary, the love of posterity or that of one's contemporaries; his provisional, punning decision is that "posterity...to me seems but a dubious kind of reed/To lean on for support in any way" (XII.18). A related aspect of performance points to the pleasure that writing involves for the person doing the making or the performing. As the passages I considered earlier should have made clear, the writing of Don Juan demanded a moment by moment participation of the poet that, because of the attentiveness, knowledge and sheer poetic skill that it presupposes, often comes very close to what might be termed, with no moral intimations, showing off. Byron focuses upon the joyous elements of performance in a metaphor he identifies as "the moral of this composition/If people would but see its real drift" (VI.88). He writes:

> "The nightingale that sings with the deep thorn,
> Which fable places in her breast of wail,
> Is lighter far of heart and voice than those
> Where headlong passions form their proper woes."
> (VI.87)

The poem avoids the usual interpretations of the legend (see Sidney's sonnets on "The Nightingale" in <u>Astrophel and Stella</u>, or Shakespeare's <u>The Rape of Lucrece</u>) for a conception very similar to one Marvell proposes in "Upon Appleton House" when he writes "The nightingale does here make choice/To sing the trials of her voice." With it, Byron distinguishes between the pain that poetry might 'express' and the joy that comes with 'expressing' that pain.

Yet Byron also understands that a conception of poetry as an occasion for soaring and pleasurable performances, or one that presents it as a gallery or theater wherein the dilemmas of the flesh, the passage of time, the strictures of involvement and immediacy, and the deprivations of ordinary life are resolved before a loving and applauding audience, can quickly and easily pass into a sentimentality that would smother literature beneath another kind of humanistic cant. At the core of each is a cup drawn from Lethe, a disremembering of all one finally knows: "and what know <u>you</u>,/Except perhaps that you were born to die?" More often, then, his attitude towards literary <u>hubris</u> approaches a remark Beckett made in a conversation with Aidan Higgins.

Higgins paraphrases: "Writing style, that vanity, he compared to a bow tie about a throat cancer."[11] <u>Don Juan</u> is replete with denunciations of any kind of vanity, which usually take a form similar to this:

> "'Where is the world?' cries Young at eighty.
>   'Where
>   The world in which a man was born?' Alas!
> Where is the world of eight years past? 'Twas
>   there--
>   I look for it--'tis gone, a globe of glass,
> Cracked, shivered, vanished, scarcely gazed on, ere
>   A silent change dissolves the glittering mass.
> Statesman, chiefs, orators, queens, patriots, kings,
> And dandies, all are gone on the wind's wings.
>   (XI.76)

Yet Byron does not even propose this informed, tenacious, almost Senecan gloom as a conclusion. Again Saturn's children are present at the Titan's table as he withdraws his attack upon literary vanity with this gentle boast: "But still I am, or was, a pretty poet."

Notes

Chapter I

1 All references to Byron's poetry in this chapter, unless specified otherwise, are to, Lord Byron, The Complete Poetical Works, ed. Jerome J. McGann (New York: Oxford University Press, 1980). Afterwards L B C P W.

2 Preface to Childe Harold's Pilgrimage in L B C P W, Vol. II, p. 6.

3 W. B. Yeats, The Autobiography of William Butler Yeats (New York: Macmillan, 1965), p. 365.

4 George Orwell, "Inside the Whale," in A Collection of Essays by George Orwell (New York and London: Harcourt Brace Jovanovich, 1953), p. 227.

5 All references to Don Juan are to the volume edited by T. G. Steffan, E. Steffan, and W. W. Pratt (Middlesex England: Penguin Books Ltd., 1973).

6 Jerome J. McGann, Don Juan in Context (Chicago and London: The University of Chicago Press, 1976), p. 123.

7 Robert Frost in Writers at Work: The Paris Review Interviews, Second Saves, ed. George Plimpton (New York: Viking, 1963), p. 39.

8 T. S. Eliot in "Andrew Marvell," in Selected Prose of T. S. Eliot, ed. Frank Kermode (New York: Harcourt Brace Jovanovich, Farrar Straus and Giroux, 1975), p. 170.

9 W. B. Yeats in A Vision (New York: Macmillan, 1969), pp. 148-149.

10 Quotations are from the version which was printed in Hours of Idleness, unless specified otherwise.

11 L B C P W Vol. I, p. 382.

12 Robert F. Gleckner, Byron and the Ruins of Paradise (Baltimore: The John Hopkins Press, 1967).

13 Written in 1806, but first published in 1832.

14 Written in 1808; first published in Imitations and Translations from the Ancient and Modern Classics, ed. J. C. Hobhouse.

15 Emily Bronte, Wuthering Heights (Middlesex, England: Penquin Books Ltd., 1979), p. 365.

16 L B C P W Vol. I, pp. 31-34.

17 L B C P W Vol. I, p. 379.

18 Richard Rogers and Lorenz Hart, "This Can't Be Love" (1938).

19 L B C P W Vol. I, p. 373.

20 L B C P W Vol. I, p. 34.

21 Written in 1807, but first published in 1832.

22 Northrop Frye in "Lord Byron" in *Fables of Identity* (New York: Harcourt Brace Jovanovich, 1963), p. 174.

23 Letter to William Bankes, 6 March 1807, in *Letters and Journals*, ed. Leslie Marchand (Cambridge: Harvard University Press, 1973), p. 111.

Chapter II

1 There are at least three ways to read *Childe Harold's Pilgrimage*--as a single poem of four Cantos, as two separate poems (I and II; III and IV), and as three separate poems (I and II; III; and IV). I lean toward the second of these. This essay, however, is concerned with the first two Cantos only. All references are to *Lord Byron, The Complete Poetical Works*, ed. Jerome J. McGann (New York: Oxford University Press, 1980), afterwards L B C P W.

2 Other speakers include Harold's page, his yeoman, and the anonymous singers of "Tambourgi! Tambourgi!"

3 Also see "To Inez," stanza 5.

4 Ernest Hartley Coleridge, ed. *The Works of Lord Byron*, Vol. II (New York: Charles Scribner's Sons, 1899), p. 65.

5 I acknowledge my debt to L B C P W Vol. II, p. 273.

6 Jerome J. McGann, *Fiery Dust* (Chicago and London: University of Chicago Press, 1968), p. 272.

7 James Merrill, *Scripts for the Pageant* (New York: Athenaeum, 1980), p. 16.

8 James Agee, *Agee on Film* (New York: McDowell and Abolensky, 1958), p. 16.

9 I quote from Byron's letter to Dallas, 11 October 1811.

10 The number of deaths in the poem is not entirely clear. Is the friend that is mourned in II.9 the same as I.91-92? Are there two? Three? More? In II.96 Byron writes, "All thou

couldst have of mine, stern Death! thou hast;/The Parent, Friend, and now the more than Friend." Hence my reference to the death of a second friend at the end of Canto II.

Chapter III

1 All references to *Don Juan* are to the edition edited by T. G. Steffan, E. Steffan and W. W. Pratt (Middlesex, England: Penguin Books Ltd., 1973).

2 John Wain, *Essays on Literature and Ideas* (Toronto and London: Macmillan and Co., Ltd., 1962), p. 48.

3 Helen Gardner, "*Don Juan*," "The London Magazine," Vol. 5, No. 7 (July, 1958) pp. 58-65.

4 The terms of this argument, as elaborated here and elsewhere in the essay, were suggested by Francis Bacon's discussion of the "Idols of the Theater" in *Novum Organum* (1620), Richard Poirier's analysis of self-parody and performance in the fiction of Joyce, Pynchon, Borges, Barth, and Mailer in *The Performing Self* (New York: Oxford University Press, 1971) and Robert Garris's *The Dickens Theater* (London: Oxford University Press, 1965).

5 Elizabeth French Boyd, *Byron's Don Juan* (New Jersey: Rutgers University Press, 1945), p. 120.

6 Andras Horn, *Byron's Don Juan and the Eighteenth-Century English Novel* (Hungary, 1962), *passim*.

7 A full discussion of this point is not among the concerns of this essay. For a more just treatment of the relationships between these examples of scientific and philosophical prose and certain early novels (but with no discussion of the place of *Don Juan* within a tradition of self-conscious narratives) see Richard Pierce, "Enter the frame," *Triquarterly*, No. 30 (Spring 1974), pp. 71-82 and Robert Alter, *Partial Magic* (Berkeley: University of California Press, 1975), *passim*.

8 The phrase is Stephan Koch's, in reference to Andy Warhol: *Stargazer* (U.S.A.: Praeger Publishers, Inc., 1973), p. 5. For a Byronic appropriation of Koch's language see: Andy Warhol, *The Philosophy of Andy Warhol* (U.S.A.: Harcourt, Brace, Jovanovich, 1975), p. 10.

9 I was using the word before I was aware of Jerome J. McGann's *Don Juan in Context*. Oddly, I was thinking of the same "Ordinary Language Philosophy" that McGann found so important. for his study of *Don Juan*.

10 Paul West, *Byron and the Spoiler's Art* (New York: St. Martin's Press, 1975), p. 10.

11 "Profile of Aidan Higgins" in *The Guardian* (October 11, 1971.

Bibliography

Agee, James. *Agee on Film*. New York: McDowell and Abolensky, 1958.

Boyd, Elizabeth French. *Byron's Don Juan*. New Jersey: Rutgers University Press, 1945.

Bronte, Emily. *Wuthering Heights*. Middlesex, England: Penguin Books, Ltd., 1975.

Coleridge, Ernest Hartley, ed. *The Works of Lord Byron*. New York: Charles Scribner's Sons, 1899.

Frye, Northrop. *Fables of Identity*. New York: Harcourt Brace Jovanovich, 1963.

Gardner, Helen. "Don Juan." *The London Magazine*, 5, No. 7 (1958), pp. 58-65.

Kermode, Frank, ed. *Selected Prose of T. S. Eliot*. New York: Harcourt Brace Jovanovich, Farrar Straus and Giroux, 1975.

Koch, Stephen. *Stargazer*. U.S.A.: Praeger Publishers, Inc., 1973.

McGann, Jerome J. *Don Juan in Context*. Chicago and London: The University of Chicago Press, 1976.

_____. *Fiery Dust*. Chicago and London: University of Chicago Press, 1968.

McGann, Jerome J., ed. *Lord Byron, The Complete Poetical Works*. New York: Oxford University Press, 1980.

Marchand, Leslie, ed. *Byron's Letters and Journals*. Cambridge: Harvard University Press, 1973.

Merrill, James. *Scripts for the Pageant*. New York: Athenaeum, 1980.

Orwell, George. *A Collection of Essays by George Orwell*. New York and London: Harcourt Brace Jovanovich, 1953.

Steffan, T. G., et. al., eds. *Don Juan*. Middlesex, England: Penguin Books Ltd., 1973.

Wain, John. *Essays on Literature and Ideas*. Toronto and London: Macmillan and Co., Ltd., 1962.

West, Paul. *Byron and the Spoiler's Art*. New York: St. Martin's Press, 1975.

Wiencek, Henry Scott. *Acts of God*. New York: Davenport and Co., Ltd., 1952.

For Product Safety Concerns and Information please contact our EU
representative GPSR@taylorandfrancis.com
Taylor & Francis Verlag GmbH, Kaufingerstraße 24, 80331 München, Germany

www.ingramcontent.com/pod-product-compliance
Lightning Source LLC
Chambersburg PA
CBHW070300230426
43664CB00014B/2586